Business Development

Andreas Kohne

Business Development

Processes, Methods and Tools

Second Edition

Andreas Kohne
Hessisch Oldendorf, Germany

ISBN 978-3-658-38843-0   ISBN 978-3-658-38844-7   (eBook)
https://doi.org/10.1007/978-3-658-38844-7

Responsible Editor: Petra Steinmueller
This Springer Vieweg imprint is published by the registered company Springer Fachmedien Wiesbaden GmbH, part of Springer Nature.
The registered company address is: Abraham-Lincoln-Str. 46, 65189 Wiesbaden, Germany

I dedicate this book to my wife Linda.

Preface to the Second Edition

What do mice and people looking for cheese in a maze have to do with Business Development? Spencer Johnsen uses exactly this metaphor in his successful book "Who moved my cheese" to encourage permanent change; the main task of Business Development (cf. [22]).

The story is about two mice and two people. They live together in a labyrinth. There one day they find a room filled with delicious cheese. Both the mice and the humans eat the cheese every day and enjoy it. While the humans make it a routine to eat cheese in just this one room, the mice, on the other hand, quickly notice that the cheese is getting less and less, and in time they go in search of new food sources in the maze. After some time, they find another chamber filled with even tastier cheese. The humans, however, remain in the first chamber and one day find that all the cheese has been eaten. They are annoyed beyond measure, since they had laid out their lives to find cheese in this chamber. One of the two people, after a period of pondering and agonizing, realizes that their situation has fundamentally changed and that they must adapt; otherwise, they will starve. He overcomes his fear and begins to search for new food sources in the labyrinth as well. The first attempts remain fruitless. But after some time, he too finds the chamber with the new cheese.

History shows very clearly that no one can rely on the same conditions prevailing tomorrow as they do today. Only those who look around, seize opportunities, and do not stand still will find something new and lucrative.

LEGO would still be selling wooden toys today, Nintendo would be producing card games, and Amazon would be one online bookseller among many. Companies must accept that ongoing digitization and globalization, disruptive innovations, and global crises or wars can change customer needs, supply chains, and entire markets overnight. Those who adapt to this and react promptly and flexibly will also be able to operate successfully on the market in the future.

Business Development offers a solution to precisely this challenge. With the right processes, methods, and tools, which are described in this book, Business Development ensures that a company with its products and services grows with the market and the needs of the customers.

The second revised and expanded edition of this book describes key performance indicators (KPIs) that are important for Business Development. It explains why a crisis can also be an opportunity and presents current, digital business models that are relevant for every company. With the Gartner Hype Cycle, McKinsey's "Three Horizons Model", and the innovation map of the company board of innovation, further tools for Business Development are presented. A detailed interview with Björn Radde (Vice President of Digital Experience at T-Systems) complements the book and rounds it off with quotes from science and business.

As the man in the story searches for new cheese, he summarizes his experiences and knowledge gained in the search and writes them on the walls of the labyrinth as a reminder for himself and for his friend. On one wall he writes: "What would you do if you were not afraid?" In this spirit, I wish you at all times the courage to leave the familiar "environment" and embark on a successful search for something new.

Hessisch Oldendorf   Dr. Andreas Kohne
May 2022

Contents

About the Author

Dr. Andreas Kohne.
(Photo courtesy of Materna
Information & Commu-
nications SE, Dortmund,
Germany,
2022)

Andreas Kohne As an expert in innovation, transformation, and communication, Andreas Kohne publishes relevant expertise in a concise and understandable way. His publications are standard international reading in business and science and appear in German and English language.

The author works as a Business Development Manager in the IT industry and guides companies and public authorities on their way through digitalization.

As a sought-after speaker, trainer, and consultant, Andreas Kohne imparts practical expertise. With a successful mix of expertise, interaction, and motivation, he travels internationally as a tech translator. In doing so, he succeeds in illustrating complex digital structures and processes in a generally understandable way.

Andreas Kohne studied computer science and business administration at the Technical University of Dortmund (Germany), where he also earned a doctorate in computer science.

He lives with his wife near Hanover, Germany.
info@andreaskohne.de
www.andreaskohne.de

List of Figures

Introduction

1

Abstract

The business world is changing faster and faster. The digitization, globalization, and technologcalization of the markets are progressing faster and faster. Companies that want to remain successful in the marketplace at this high speed must constantly adapt to changing circumstances and customer needs. This is exactly what Business Development supports. It optimizes individual divisions, products, or services and permanently aligns them to market needs. In addition to involving employees in these changes, a successful change management is needed, which helps to communicate and anchor the necessary changes. At the same time, the stakeholders of the respective products and areas must be informed at all times and involved in important decisions. To make all this possible, a corporate culture must be created, for which change and optimization is the norm.

We live in a time of constant and ever-faster change. All-encompassing digitization is becoming ever faster and affecting all areas of life. This affects the private as well as the business life. The Internet has completely changed communication and global trade in less than a decade and there is no end in sight. Cloud computing and mobile devices, such as tablets and smartphones, have become an integral part of everyday life and are changing the way people communicate with each other and how companies communicate with their customers. Entire value chains are emerging on the Internet, resulting in new business models.

This rapid development also brings changes in the expectations of customers and employees to products, services, and the way in which people work and communicate. Employees' expectations of their company are summarized by the term Consumerization. This means that the employees in the company want to work productively with mobile devices as well as social media with the same naturalness as in the private life. Transformations in the business world can be seen, for example, with the trend of BYOD (bring your own device). For example, BYOD allows private smartphones and tablets to be used as normal work equipment

© Springer Fachmedien Wiesbaden GmbH, part of Springer Nature 2023
A. Kohne, *Business Development*,
https://doi.org/10.1007/978-3-658-38844-7_1

and to use in-house services such as e-mail, calendars, and data services (see [17]). This is only a company internal change.

The expectations of customers are increasing with the ongoing digitization. More than ever before, products and services should be constantly considered and adapted, and new products must be positioned faster and cheaper in the marketplace. Instead, the traditional development methods should be thrown overboard and be replaced with contemporary and agile methods. If such a permanent process of change does not take place, the traditional enterprise and its business models can be overtaken on the left and on the right and left wide behind new markets. Nowadays, there is no big deal in the way of putting Internet-based businesses on the map, potentially counting millions of users worldwide overnight. This new situation in the business world presents many companies with traditional business models with great challenges. The business cycles have changed and shortened rapidly. Today, it is no longer uncommon for an Internet start-up to become a global giant with huge numbers of users within 6 months starting from total unknownness, only to be swallowed up by an even larger company or investor and then completely disappear again. These events are referred to as disruptive changes (see [13]). In such a short time, these companies can cause massive damage to the traditional markets and possibly even ruin whole companies. For example, consider the launching of the mp3 standard for music playback. Almost overnight, an entire industry was razed to the ground and it is still in parts still trying to recover. Music players such as cassettes and CD players were suddenly no longer needed. Nevertheless, your complete music collection could be carried around at any time. But not only the makers of the players had a massive problem. Also, the producers of the records faced massive sales losses. In the meantime, music download portals are established, which offer access to vast amounts of music at a fixed rate. The same trend has been evident in the movie industry for a few years now. Here, the ever-advancing Internet broadband expansion is steadily increasing the number of users of streaming services. This trend will in the near future also completely change the way television and movies are consumed.

As well as digitization, the globalization and internationalization of markets continue. The worldwide logistics networks are becoming ever more finely tuned and the speed of international traffic continues to increase. Likewise, research-driven progress continues in all areas from new product development to manufacturing.

These examples are only two among many. The digitization and internationalization of markets can wipe out or fundamentally change entire industries from one day to the next. Losers are often the old-established companies that do not expect that a small start-up could pull off their entire clientele within a very short time. The winners of this new era are those companies that are able to recognize such changes and react to them very quickly and spontaneously reinvent themselves when in doubt.

Especially entrepreneurs who have been very successful in the past think that a (radical) change in their value proposition is out of the question and often you can hear the phrase "It has always been like this...". This is an argument against change, but change is urgently needed. A study by DIM (German Institute for Marketing) shows that a once-good idea, which was successfully sold, is worth nothing in the medium to long term. It states that 80% of all businesses fail in the first 5 years. In the first 10 years, even 24 out of 25 companies disappear. The reason is simple: not enough new customers could be won in the medium term and existing customers could no longer be bound to the company with updated offers.

That is why any business, whether it's a service or product company, requires constant innovation, change, and adaptation to new market realities and customer needs. For this change to succeed and last, it must be done in a well-ordered and plannable manner. Here lies the basic idea of Business Development. The Business Development team within a corporation is responsible for ensuring that the products or services offered are optimally tailored to a given target customer area. In addition, Business Development is responsible for the permanent adaptation of product portfolios to changing market conditions. This also includes, for example, the aspect of partner management. In doing so, the partners of a company are selected and controlled in a targeted manner, so that together more business is created.

Business Development comes classically from IT-related companies. There, the sweeping changes in the last decades were the biggest. In the meantime, Business Development has become established in many industries, as it brings many benefits to companies that are not purely IT-savvy. For example, in the areas of biotechnology, chemistry, and medicine, Business Development is being heavily relied on, as internationalization and the ever greater degree of prefabrication of low-cost supply products demand a completely different business. In general, Business Development is essential for all companies in all areas. There is no fixed value for the number of employees. Even companies that have just completed their start-up phase will have to adapt their products permanently to the market. Whether a separate business unit is founded or the task is carried out by the sales or marketing manager, for example, depends on many individual factors, which are not taken into consideration here.

This book goes on to introduce Business Development in detail, showing you how to set up and optimally operate Business Development in your company and which disciplines need to be taken into account. For this purpose, the book is structured as follows: First, in Chap. 1, Business Development is defined and differentiated from other business areas. Furthermore, the most important stakeholders and the necessary corporate culture are examined in detail. Then, in Chap. 2, Business Development is presented in detail. A precise distinction is made between the role of the Business Development Manager, the organizational unit, and the actual process. Subsequently, the topic of the portfolio is explained in Chap. 3 and the impact that Business Development has on forward-looking portfolio development is described. The next chapter is dedicated to the area of resources Chap. 4. Here, skill management, the management of internal and external resources, the topic of mergers and acquisitions, and the topic of controlling are discussed. This is followed by an examination of the target market in Chap. 5. In this section, the topics of market observation, risk analysis, market segmentation, and internationalization are addressed. Subsequently, the heart of Business Development, the market cultivation strategy, is presented in detail in Chap. 6. Among other things, this covers pricing, the sales concept, the partner concept, the marketing concept, and sales enablement. Further on, Business Development is shown in action in a fictitious case study in Chap. 7. Chapter 8 contains a detailed interview with Björn Radde (Vice President Digital Experience, T-Systems) on the topic of Business Development. Finally, Chap. 9 shows the six steps to successful Business Development. The book is rounded off in Chap. 10 with quotes from science and business.

Please note that this book aims to describe the field of Business Development as holistically as possible. To this end, the concept of Business Development is described in such a way that it can be applied to all types of businesses. For this reason, no consistent distinction is made between product and service in the following.

But for now, I hope you enjoy this book and that it helps you to gain a comprehensive impression of the topic of Business Development. No matter if you are a manager who wants to introduce or optimize Business Development in your company or if you are already working in this area or will be doing so in the future, I hope this book will provide you with answers and suggestions and help you to shape and develop your business in a future-proof and customer-oriented way.

1.1   Business Development

In recent years, Business Development has become the key driver for changes and adjustments in many industries. Business Development is not a clearly defined task or a clearly defined role. It is rather a collection of different approaches that, when used properly, help to permanently align a company with the wishes and requirements of the customers and to achieve the highest possible market penetration. This often leads to misunderstandings. Business Development tasks are always dedicated to a specific business, product, or service rather than trying to develop the whole company. This would be called Corporate Development, which refers to the strategic corporate planning, optimization, and expansion of a company. Another term that would better describe the task would be Business Field Development. Here, it becomes clear that Business Development optimizes and expands individual areas of a given company.

The tasks of Business Development are roughly as follows (see [33])—Business Development should

1. satisfy existing, unexpressed market needs;
2. bring new technology, products, or services to the market;
3. break up or improve existing markets with a new business model; and
4. create or explore brand new markets.

Normally, Business Development works in the areas (1) to (3). Often, these areas also work together with marketing, production, and research departments. Point 4) should not go unmentioned here, but it is reserved for the very big companies of a particular industry, which can muster the time and the necessary money to create a whole new market with new products. Apple is certainly a good example here.

Example

Prior to the launch of the first iPad in 2010, there was no market for tablet computers at all, and there were virtually no smartphones in the year before this year. As early as 2013, the number of mobile home devices (smartphones and tablets) exceeded the sales of classic PCs and notebooks. So it is possible to have such a success, but normally it is about business changes on a smaller scale. ◄

Many, especially smaller companies, often face the problem that they only have a small number of revenue carriers (products and/or services) in their portfolio and can often place these only with a very small number of customers. This can have many reasons. For example, an IT consulting firm will first acquire assignments in the nearby environment; otherwise, there will be additional costs for travel and expenses and the company may not even be familiar with certain localities. It even happens that 80% of the total turnover of a company is achieved with only one customer. There is thus a very high dependence on this customer. But even when doing business with other customers, it is never an advantage for a customer to be overly important to a given business. This is, for example, a classic starting point for Business Development.

One of the central tasks of Business Development is to win new customers for the available products and to expand existing customer relationships. In order to achieve this, the products offered should be optimally geared to the needs of the market and (ideally) support the customers in a very important situation or solve a central problem for the customer. It is therefore not simply done by turning up sales. There are fundamental changes and adjustments to be made to the products and the way they are sold. Of course, the sales aspect plays a major role in Business Development. There is a need to constantly open up new customers and possibly new markets and to supply existing customers with other products of that company. This is called cross and up-selling. In the process of up-selling, a customer buys more of an existing product, and in cross-selling, additional products from the portfolio are sold to an existing customer.

This permanent adaptation and optimization of the product portfolio are not usual for many companies. It has been working with a successful product in a stable market. Unfortunately, the markets have been changing faster and faster in recent years, and there is no end in sight. The change, driven by digitization, mechanization, and globalization, is likely to increase even more. Quite overnight, entire markets can now be overturned or even completely wiped out. These drastic changes are called Big Bang Disruptions (see [13])—Disruptive changes are essentially massive market changes that are driven by new technology or the profitable combination of existing technologies into a completely new product. In particular, the combination of existing technologies with new solutions basically costs nothing anymore, as more or less hazardous digital products (hardware and software) can be made into new packages without consuming large costs or production resources. You can be more or less sure that somewhere in the world at this point in time someone is working on something that threatens your business tomorrow. Nowadays, Business Development is imperative because most companies cannot adapt quickly enough on their own. It's an engine that keeps the permanent change in motion and is constantly developing new ideas and balancing them with the market. In the normal case, changes are caused by great pain. The alternatives to this are big goals. Business Development is responsible for working with the management to develop new visions that will lead the company into a profitable future. Think of the famous sentence of Helmut Schmidt (former German Chancellor): "If you have visions, you should go to the doctor". So watch out for visions that are based on data and facts rather than on ideas that do not target given market needs. For this, large agility in the company is necessary. This flexibility in the adaptation and development of new ideas is the responsibility of Business Development. A central task of Business Development is to ensure that the change and adaptation of the company become normality. This is implemented by accompanied Innovation Management, which permanently challenges the status quo and generates market- and customer-oriented products. This requires a concrete process, which should be carried out permanently. Exactly this process is described in detail in Sect. 2.5.

There are also a few things to keep in mind with all the changes that require a closer look. In some cases, it can pay off to prove a long breath. Instead of giving up after a short time, in which a new product has probably not been accepted in the marketplace as it was planned, it sometimes pays off to wait a bit more. Fast change is good, but it should not be at the expense of healthy and organic growth of companies, ideas, and products. Thus, a close look at the entire portfolio and the market conditions is also a central task of Business Development. An important task is to closely monitor the lifecycle of each portfolio item and to cancel and remove items that are no longer up-to-date and no longer profitable to produce or sell. Portfolio Management is discussed in Chap. 3.

Any change in the portfolio should of course be targeted. This means that new products will only be introduced if there is a concrete and rated market. It is very helpful to align new products and services to concrete bottlenecks of the customer. Section 2.5.1 will detail on the Bottleneck Focused Strategy. This strategy can then be used to optimize and tailor customer solutions and to constantly control and consolidate the portfolio.

Business Development is responsible for a permanent market observation. Current trends in the market must be recorded and evaluated at an early stage. In the process, it must be discovered which innovations and which technologies are future-oriented and which are in line with the company and its business. Thus, a solid market observation is essential. In addition, Business Development Managers should have an ongoing exchange with customers to find out what they are currently dealing with, what challenges and problems they face, and where they need support. Again, caution is advised, because it is not always enough to respond to customer requests. These are very individual problems and a vision should be created from the wishes of all customers, which can help the company to reposition and optimize existing products. Often this is not enough. Customers also expect manufacturers or service providers to come up with novel ideas. Henry Ford recognized this problem and summed it up in his famous quote: "If I had asked people what they wanted, they would have said faster horses". He wanted to say that customers are often limited in their thinking to their own experience and thus demand no innovation. But this is precisely the task of Business Development: to develop innovative solutions that meet a specific need in the market.

In addition to communication with customers, the communication and control of partners, external suppliers, and service providers are a central function of Business Development. The business has become more fragmented these days and only a few companies are completely independent of suppliers. These can be suppliers of raw materials, component suppliers, logistics partners, hardware and software partners, distribution partners (inland and abroad), freelancers, and near and offshoring partners. All of these partners must be selected according to defined criteria, cooperative agreements must be concluded and supervised, price negotiations must be conducted, joint business plans must be drawn up, and, possibly, even acquired new customers together. All this must be done with a central strategy. Business Development is the ideal unit to accomplish these tasks by establishing and refining a strategic system around its own innovations and existing products.

Due to the constant acceleration and internationalization of markets, there are large amounts of company consolidations in many sectors. Many companies, on their own, no longer produce the desired organic growth. Thus, they strengthen themselves with acquisitions. This area is often referred to as mergers and acquisitions (M & A). It is about the intelligent search, evaluation, and selection of possible target companies that complement the portfolio optimally. Exactly this pre-selection is ideally placed in Business Development. Depending on how your company is set up, the entire M & A process can be anchored in the Business Development process. This leads from the concrete financial evaluation of the goal over the actual purchase up to the integration into the existing enterprise after the purchase is completed. In Sect. 4.5, this area is presented in detail.

Before you implement a Business Development in your company, there are a few things to keep in mind. First, clarify for yourself the purpose of your company. Why are you there? What is the benefit for your customers? How exactly do you help your customers? These fundamental considerations later help in the strategy process to focus on the core competencies and to develop the company in a direction that is also credible. The most important question is certainly the question of the reason of your company. Once this is resolved, the rest will be self-evident. A strong and credible answer to the "why" will help you in every conversation with your customers and partners, as your intentions are clear and your added value can be clearly shown to the client. The customer can therefore identify more easily with your company and the products (see [43]).

In the concrete implementation of Business Development, make sure that the basic idea behind it is that of lean management. This means that you implement lean processes that help you to be agile in the business and to adapt to changes. Further, these processes should be lightweight for flexibility and speed of action. Also, keep in mind that the market and your customers should be the center of all considerations. So be prepared to meet the demands of the market and pay attention to even the smallest changes in order to adapt quickly.

Finally, the question arises as to who is responsible for Business Development in an enterprise. Once again, there is no clear answer, as this task is interpreted differently from company to company, with different rights and interests, and, of course, depending on the size and structure of a company. In smaller companies, this position (consciously or unconsciously) oftentimes is held by the CEO. In larger companies, this task is often taken over by the sales manager or it is also found in marketing. The larger a company is and the more diverse the tasks of a company, the more likely it is that there is a separate team or even a separate department for the topic of Business Development. From which persons such a team is then built depends again strongly on the desired goal. An exact definition of the role of a Business Development Manager can be found in Sect. 2.2.

Whatever applies to your business, you first begin to define the function of Business Development. Establish concrete goals that you want to achieve. Should costs be reduced in a certain area? Should sales be increased with one product? Do you want to hedge or even extend your market position? Should the EBIT (Earnings Before Taxes And Interest) or the gain be increased? Should existing or new products be used to open new markets or expand existing ones? Do you want to revise your sales mix? Should a new growth strategy be worked out for a given area? And so on and so forth. The purpose of Business Development is to professionally evaluate one's own business in order to derive a clear strategy for individual areas. Decide on what an organizational structure might look like in your company. Remember the Bauhaus principle: Form follows function. Do you need a dedicated team or can the task (still) be carried out in unison (together with the managing director, sales manager, marketing manager, department manager, etc.)? Is even a reorganization or restruction necessary in parts of the company? Should Business Development only be set up for a dedicated area, or potentially be responsible for all areas of the company? Only after you have clarified these questions in detail, you can deliberately think about the structure of Business Development in your company. How a Business Development organizational unit might look exactly like is described in detail in Sect. 2.4.

As you have seen so far, Business Development is an extensive, responsible, and important task. Business Development provides a central, permanent change for your company and products. Be careful to implement or restructure your Business Development so that you do not place the person, team, or division as a paper tiger. This means that Business Development requires extensive powers of attorney in order to be able to implement the tasks presented. This is the only way Business Development can grow to its full potential. Otherwise, the department can no longer be an idea giver whose ideas may never be implemented. So if you want a real change, pay close attention to this point. Also, make sure that Business Development is controlled by management and that far-reaching decisions can only be made in collaboration with management.

1.2   Business Change Goals

In order to adapt to new market situations, companies must constantly change. This task has to be wanted by the management and supported purposefully. Business Development can help in many areas. According to Narasimhan et al., there are five strategic goals that a business change can have (see [32]):

1. *Global Presence:* The aim is to internationalize operations and increase global market coverage. Business Development can assist with global market observation and find profitable markets. In doing so, international trends and social changes should be included.
2. *Customer Focus:* The goal of this change is to provide bespoke customer solutions and actively respond to customer needs. Through targeted market research and customer surveys, Business Development can filter out market trends, wishes, and needs and make targeted contributions to the development process.
3. *Innovation:* New ideas for products or business models are to be developed. For example, this can be done in collaboration with partners (e.g., research companies) or Business Development.
4. *Nimbleness:* Here, the business processes should be adapted and made more agile. This applies above all to corporate strategy, operations, and corporate culture. These are classic tasks that relate to the company as such and are not directly related to the products, customers, and target markets. Thus, this is a task for Corporate Development.
5. *Sustainability:* This increasingly important goal is becoming more and more important to many companies as end users increasingly pay attention. In concrete terms, it deals with the use of resources, environmental friendliness, and social responsibility. Here, too, Business Development can use targeted market observation to determine important market and environmental trends, to ask about customers' wishes, and to integrate the results into product development and production.

Achieving the goals described here requires a change in processes, rules, procedures, and habits in many areas. That's why successful change management is very important. The following chapter explains the topic in detail.

1.3   Change Management

Having already described the most important tasks of Business Development, it should also be mentioned here that it is also a non-negligible task of Business Development to communicate the changes in the company and to ensure that the changes really be implemented. These changes can be, for example, the announcement of a new product or a new partner, a new sales approach for an existing product, or the explanation of a new business model. All this is summarized under the generic term Change Management. This is a targeted approach in which far-reaching changes in a company are communicated and implemented (see [3]). Often these change processes are also accompanied by the internal marketing department with appropriate communication measures.

For a successful change management, some important tasks have emerged. In the following, the twelve success factors according to Gerkhard and Frey are briefly summarized (see [29]):

1. *Comprehensive Symptom Description and Organizational Analysis:* In the first process, the causes must first be explained and described. Be as specific as possible and do not mince words, even if it's your own company. Clarify questions such as: Where is the company now? How is it structured? How is the market tackled? How are the customer needs addressed? Why is a change necessary at all?
2. *Define visions and goals:* Afterward, deconstruct from the initial situation a vision that describes exactly what your company will look like after the change. What will your product look like? How and in which markets is it positioned through which channels? Do the turnover and profit figures differ?
3. *Common Problem Awareness:* In the next step, create a common problem awareness among everyone involved. It is important to note that all stakeholders (see Sect. 1.4) are involved from the beginning and are permanently informed about the further process.
4. *Leadership Coordinator/Supporter:* Seek advocates of change in all key positions and make them ambassadors who set a good example and help you bring about change in the business. Make sure that these employees serve as multipliers in their respective areas and convince as many others as possible of the benefits of change. As a result, you gain acceptance faster with all those involved. Please note that above all the management has to support the change and is clearly behind you. Otherwise, the project is implausible.
5. *Communication:* Please think from the beginning of a comprehensive communication. It's best to set up a communication strategy right at the beginning of the change together with your internal marketing. This ensures that all employees have all the important information at all times. The area of communication is discussed again in detail in Sect. 2.5.9.
6. *Time Management:* Many changes are mission critical, or at least very important to the business. Make sure that you have the most concrete timetable possible from the outset and that you constantly align with reality and readjust existing delays. Note that you install sufficient buffers, check the plan permanently, and balance it with reality. Communicate deviations and develop alternate scenarios. This is the only way to ensure that the change project is completed in a timely manner.
7. *Project organization and responsibilities:* No project should be started without a specific organization and without clear responsibilities. While this is obvious, projects often fail to do so. There must be exactly one project leader who manages and is responsible for the project. Depending on the size and scope of the project, further employees will be added and clear responsibilities will be assigned. Each task must be given a clear

budget, a clear goal, and a deadline when the (sub-) project must be completed. For the precise organization and execution of projects, there are a wide variety of procedure models, which are often individually adapted and adjusted by each company. The only important thing is that you have a concrete approach with clear structures and a clean documentation.

8. *Help for self-help, qualification, and resources:* Talk to all the stakeholders permanently. Explain the necessity of the project over and over again. Make sure that all employees have enough resources, such as time and budget; otherwise, displeasure will arise that can continue on through the whole project. Involve all stakeholders and make sure everyone pulls together.

9. *Quick Wins:* During a change project, it is very important to present the first results quickly and achieve intermediate goals. These are called quick wins. A quick win at the beginning of a project sends a positive message and helps employees to recognize the benefits of the project more quickly. If you plan a big change over a long period of time in a quiet room and only rumors of potential effects are distributed, it can quickly endanger the project. So right at the beginning, look for a positive intermediate destination that you can reach relatively quickly and communicate this via suitable media within the company.

10. *Flexibility in the process:* Keep in mind with all the planning that you are flexible within the process. Do not rigidly work the project to plan, but adapt yourself and the project depending on the situation to the conditions that arise. This guarantees that in the meantime, the resulting (external) changes will be included and that your project will ultimately be successful and still based on reality.

11. *Process Monitoring/Coaching:* Monitor the process and provide help and support. This ensures that the goals are met and the change arrives at everyone. Involve a coach who can help you communicate the change to the workforce.

12. *Anchoring the change:* Ensure that the change is permanently anchored; in the minds of your employees and in the DNS of your company. After completion of the project, continue to report the results and further show the benefits. Also, if management makes the change beyond the project to the outside, show all employees the importance and sustainability of the change.

After giving a comprehensive introduction to Business Development in this chapter, the key stakeholders are described below.

1.4 Stakeholders

Business Development is not on its own. Rather, Business Development is a central task with interfaces to various areas of the company. Thus, the Business Development Managers also work with many different people from different departments. Different people have a varied interest in further development of the portfolio. All persons and groups directly or indirectly affected by Business Development are referred to as Stakeholders. Here, are a few key stakeholders. Of course, the list is not exhaustive and can vary from company to company.

- *Management:* Management has a great interest in the fact that the company is always developing and selling new and market-relevant products and services. Most of the time Business Development has been initiated by the management and reports directly to the management. In addition, it is the management that has to finally approve a new product idea before it can be transferred to production and the sales process.
- *Sales Managers:* Since the salesperson is responsible for selling the new products, at an early stage the sales management should be involved in the development and testing of new products. The distribution represents the connection to the customer and can thus also bring feedback from the market into the Business Development process. Furthermore, distribution can assist in determining the price and other structures.
- *Marketing Management:* New products have to be advertised and announced in the target market. For this purpose, a communication strategy is to be developed and implemented. To schedule appropriate campaigns in the near future, marketing should be integrated with the Business Development process.
- *Individual departments:* New products and services as well as upgrades to you offerings have to be developed for special departments. They will later make sure that the product can be produced or that the appropriate staff is available for the services. Therefore, the persons responsible for the business should be involved in the Business Development. You can help to avoid developing future products past the business reality.
- *Controlling:* Another important stakeholder is controlling. Controlling should also be included early on in the process to determine which metrics need to be measured in what way later in the sales phase and what impact this will have on the business figures. To verify that the new product arrives at the market, appropriate sales surveys must be established. It may be that the newly developed product or service has a completely novel business model and is uncontrollable with the previous controlling mechanisms. Hereby the controlling can intervene and advise early enough.
- *Customers:* An important, if not the most important, stakeholder is often forgotten. The customers with their wishes and expectations should always be the center of all considerations. Because what helps the greatest and most beautiful product, if nobody wants to buy it. It has turned out that it makes sense to carry out a precise market and customer analysis at the beginning of the Business Development process and to discuss prototypes with real customers at an early stage. This ensures that the product is not developed past the market.

After listing the most important stakeholders for the Business Development process here, the next chapter introduces the "VUCA concept".

1.5 VUCA

The world is becoming increasingly complex and interconnected. Effects of strategic decisions are increasingly difficult to predict and long-term planning has become impossible in many areas. This phenomenon is often referred to as "VUCA". The term is an acronym first coined by the American military to describe the confusing situation after the collapse of the USSR. Later, it was adopted in business and often refers to the field of digitalization. Specifically, VUCA means the following:

- *V—Volatility:* Everything around us is losing its permanence. Old business laws no longer apply. Events deliver random results and conclusions from cause to effect become impossible in parts.
- *U—Uncertainty:* Plans lose validity. Long predictions, calculations, and forecasts are overtaken by reality. The development of markets can no longer be clearly predicted.
- *C—Complexity:* Everything is intertwined. Changes to one part can lead to unpredictable results in other parts. It becomes impossible to understand and control large systems.
- *A—Ambiguity:* Nothing is clear anymore. Decisions are no longer right or wrong. Much more, "It depends". Business requirements can be paradoxical or contradictory.

The management of a company and also Business Development must be aware of this prevailing complexity and master the balancing act between optimizing the existing portfolio and innovation in an uncertain environment. In this context, knowledge gained from experience is becoming less and less important, as new, unprecedented situations need to be dealt with more frequently, requiring a completely new assessment. In some cases, there are radical changes in the markets, long-established industry laws are becoming obsolete, and today's customers are no longer necessarily tomorrow's customers. It is becoming increasingly apparent that linear thinking, planning, and action are no longer effective. It is necessary to plan for the short term and to check and correct more frequently. Basically, most long-term plans and strategies are no longer worth the paper they are printed on. According to the motto: "Planning is everything, the plan is nothing", the goals should be clearly in view and permanent readjustments should be made when the goals are reached in order to stay on the right track.

The answer to the challenges of the VUCA world is VUCA again:

- *V—Vision:* A company must have a clear goal with a strong "why". This conveys a sense of purpose, which today is more in focus than the mere product or a brand. If the goal is clear, the path can be permanently readjusted. Without a clear goal, every path looks equally good or bad.
- *U—Understanding:* Even if this is only completely possible in small areas: An attempt should be made to gain a clear understanding of the company and the target market with its requirements. It should be noted that knowledge from yesterday may already be

outdated today. It should be checked regularly whether assumptions still correspond to reality.

- **C—Clarity:** Clarity should prevail in the company. Both internally and externally. A clear strategy and goals should be established, which are then communicated internally. In addition, clear messages should be developed for customers and placed in the target markets. This prevents misunderstandings and provides support in uncertain times.
- **A—Agility:** Rigid and inflexible systems are no longer suitable for the VUCA world. From leadership, to processes, to projects: A company should be built and managed in an agile way so that it can adapt to new circumstances in a flexible and timely manner. This is how the company navigates uncertain times toward the common vision.

1.6   Ambidextry

In its original sense, Ambidextry means using both hands. This refers to the ability of a company to simultaneously optimize its existing business and build up future business. Thus, a balance must be struck between the two opposing goals of exploitation (taking advantage of existing opportunities and optimizing the current business) and Exploration (exploration of new business models and business areas as well as development of further, innovative offers) must be given (cf. [45]). Thus, the company should be efficient and innovative at the same time. To achieve this, the classic "either-or" must be exchanged for an "as-well-as" in order to be adaptable enough for new market situations in the long term.

There are three approaches to implementing this Ambidextry in a company as follows:

1. **Temporal Ambidextry:** Here, a phase of optimizing current production and sales processes and the current portfolio alternates with a phase of innovation and forward-planning. The length of the individual phases must be determined individually by each company. Phases that are too short leave little room for in-depth analysis and change. Phases that are too long delay important measures from the subsequent phase. In reality, it often turns out that a clean separation of the phases is almost impossible, since complex processes and projects are involved that are very difficult to plan in concrete terms. Thus, the phases often overlap in the case of temporal Ambidextry.

2. **Contextual Ambidextry:** Here, employees are given the opportunity to independently switch context between exploitation and exploration during working hours. The best example of this is Google's (Alphabet) 80/20 rule: Employees are allowed to spend 20% of their productive work time on innovative projects without any requirements from the company. This ensures that employees are highly motivated to do their work in the 80% and can devote themselves freely to their interests and ideas in the 20%. All sides benefit from this, because just one innovative idea from an employee can mean millions in business for the company. Well-known examples of successful ideas from the

"20% projects" are the mail service "Gmail", the map service "Google Maps", and the advertising service "AdSense", which now accounts for a large proportion of sales.

3. **Structural Ambidextry:** In this case, different business units are set up for exploration and exploitation. One unit takes care of the optimization of the current business only and the other one takes care of the innovation part. Here, it is the task of management to allow both parts to operate as independently as possible while creating common goals that pay off overall to the future viability of the company.

No matter which implementation method you choose: It will always be very difficult for management: On the one hand, customer wishes must be fulfilled in the short term in order to generate the required sales. On the other hand, new products must be developed, tested, and placed on the market with a great deal of innovative energy. To make this possible, an open and positive culture of making mistakes and learning is essential in the company. Employees and management must adapt to new circumstances and challenges, learn new things, try out new things, and learn from mistakes. This is the only way a company can remain relevant in the market in the long term. Business Development can make the decisive difference here, since it is precisely here, at the interface between portfolio and innovation management, that work is done. With a well-positioned Business Development, you are optimally positioned for a successful future.

It turns out that traditional project approaches and management processes are not designed for these conflicting goals. They require fundamentally different management in order to pursue long-term and short-term goals, to fulfill current and future customer requirements, to optimize what already exists, and at the same time to invent something new. This is where traditional systems and processes reach their limits. One possible approach to bringing together these rapid changes is agility.

1.7   Agility

According to the word, agility means maneuverability, flexibility, or mobility. Even though the topic has been on everyone's lips lately, the idea behind it is not new. The topic has been discussed since the 1970s. However, agility did not have its breakthrough until the digitalization and globalization of the corporate world.

In terms of a company, agility means that rigid and inflexible processes are actively broken down in order to be able to adapt flexibly and promptly to changing circumstances and requirements.

The agile project approach has become very popular for many years in the field of software development in the context of Scrum. Scrum is an agile development method in which the end result is broken down into many small partial results, which are then collected centrally, sorted, and processed step by step. The individual development steps are precisely defined and divided into so-called sprints. For example, a sprint always lasts 2 weeks. During these

2 weeks, the development team works through a predefined set of requirements from the so-called backlog. The big difference between classic development methods of software development with firmly defined results is that the requirements for the end product can still change during development with Scrum. This means that new findings, requirements, or ideas from the customer can still be integrated during the project and implemented on time.

This flexible approach to a project is a great advantage since in VUCA times important changes and requirements can arise spontaneously that would cause the initial plan to fail if it were not adapted at runtime. Thus, in agile projects, solutions are developed iteratively and the final result is implemented in small increments that build on each other.

Thus, the agile approach is the answer to disruption, digitalization, and globalization. Classic forms of business are no longer flexible enough to be able to react quickly to sometimes drastic changes in the market. In addition, companies are not designed to deal with Ambidextry and are often overwhelmed with the implementation (see Sect. 1.6).

Agility can also be implemented by individual teams, entire organizations, and of course in Business Development. The key is to break up rigid processes (where appropriate) and work together across all hierarchical levels to solve current problems. This requires an open culture of innovation that allows for mistakes and at the same time learns from them. Since there is no absolute knowledge, it is necessary to plan on sight, implement, and, in case of doubt, dynamically reschedule. Only at the end can a result be evaluated. Possible wrong decisions can then be analyzed in retrospect and avoided in the future.

Agility is therefore much more than just another process to be introduced in a company. Agility is an attitude or a mindset. Only with an agile corporate culture can a company act flexibly enough today and in the future to drive the development of its own business on the one hand and to be able to serve the needs of the customer optimally on the other. Business Development can also act as a driving force for innovation internally, setting a good example and exemplifying agility for the entire company.

Another approach to rapid product development is "lean business", which is described in the following chapter.

1.8   Lean Start-up Mentality

Traditionally, new products were often developed in a quiet room. They were perfected until the developers thought the products would be ready for the market. Then they were handed over to sales and marketing. The task then was to introduce these new products to the market and find corresponding buyers.

This approach is no longer the right one in the increasingly fast-moving markets. The principles of the "Lean Start-up" as presented by Eric Ries (see [39]) break with this approach. According to Ries, product development should be based on an iterative, step-by-step process. The formula "Build, Measure, Learn" is the core of the Lean Start-up. New products are to be developed quickly and tested on the market at an early stage. Customer feedback should then be quickly incorporated into the next development cycle so that the product can be optimally adapted to the target market.

This method can also be used early to determine that a product that is initially promising will never reach marketability. This is classically seen as a error or failure. In fact, it's just the honest market feedback on a new idea. This kind of failure does not need to be overstated, but to learn from the mistakes or wrong assumptions about the product or the market and to make it better next time. In a large company, such setbacks can of course be dealt with much easier than in a Start-up, which puts everything on one card. To be successful anyway, a new product must be presented to critical customers at an early stage and permanently adapted.

Failure must not be considered a total disaster. Certainly, it must not mean that product development is stopped, people are dismissed or labeled as failure. Use your customers' feedback to continue your efforts to develop optimal products that truly add value to your customers.

Use the feedback from your customers and the market, even if it is negative. It helps you to better tailor your products to the needs of your customers. Incorporate this kind of failure into the culture of your company and give yourself and your employees the freedom to be wrong. But make sure that if you fail early in the development process, you can counteract quickly and your development costs remain low. Check your hypotheses about your product, the market and customer needs early and permanently. In this way, you will be able to develop market-relevant products faster and minimize the number of failed products.

1.9   Corporate Culture

Business Development offers many advantages, as it can deal with current market changes much faster. In order for the entire company to be able to profitably implement the ideas and concepts developed in Business Development, there must also be a rethink in the minds of all employees. In order to be able to align faster with customer wishes and to recognize new technologies as a business-relevant advantage and to be able to incorporate them into the daily business, a corresponding corporate culture is needed. This culture must be shaped by the idea that the company is always the best service provider or producer for its customers. So the company has to constantly reinvent itself in order to be the best problem solver for the customer and thus to offer real added value for the customer. This will inevitably lead to success sooner or later.

In order to develop this new corporate culture, it is first of all important that it is clearly explained why the company actually exists. What does the company want to achieve? What is the vision? These statements form the core of the new culture. Based on this, you should define that your customers are always at the center of all your plans and ideas. Your customers and the market in which you have come first. With the demands of the customers, you have to adjust your portfolio. Whether it is services or products. To ensure this, your company must have a high rate of change. This is a complex task, especially for large companies and corporations, since many employees have to be taken along in this process and it may be necessary to break up old structures and simplify old processes. A picture that nicely sums up this concept is the following: Imagine that your business needs to evolve from a slow, stodgy oil tanker to a fast and agile speedboat. The goal should be that the change does not scare employees and management, but that constant change and adaptation have become the norm. To achieve this, you must ensure that all employees feel that they are part of the company and encourage them to keep their eyes and ears open, to respond to new market demands or needs, and to develop improvements. This is the only way to ensure that the aforementioned Big Bang Disruptions will not leave you empty-handed and that you will be overtaken by faster companies left and right.

These and other adjustments in your company are summarized under the term lean management. The goal is to improve yourself and the whole company and to align your business with the demands of the market. All processes from planning to production are constantly put to the test and consistently optimized. From the Japanese, the term *Kaizen* has become known for many years. The word is composed of the two words *Kai* (= change) and *Zen* (= for the better). The following are the most important principles for a lean company (see [31]:

- Orientation of activities on the customers (customer orientation).
- Concentration on your own strengths.
- Business process optimization.
- Continuous improvement of quality.
- Internal customer orientation as a corporate mission statement.
- Personal responsibility, empowerment, and teamwork.
- Decentralized, customer-oriented structures.
- Leading is service to the employee.
- Open information and feedback processes.
- Change of attitude and culture in the company (jap.: *Kaikaku*).

Business Development is the engine in this culture, which uses a well-regulated process to ensure that employees' ideas are heard, valued, and potentially implemented in the same way as ideas coming from Business Development or management. To do this, you need to make sure that your Business Development unit does not become an ivory tower, from which strange ideas are thrown into the day-to-day business. Ensure open communication between Business Development and the rest of the company.

▶   **Tip** Set up a regular roundtable where employees from different parts of your company discuss current topics and Business Development explains which projects are being worked on. By doing so, you make sure all ideas are heard and noticed.

You can also use your internal communication channels to explain current projects. For example, you can post information in your company newsletter or blog. Of course, the projects should already have a status that is communicable at the time. Position your Business Development as an important internal partner that helps the company to continue to operate successfully in the marketplace.

For your considerations, do not involve only your own company, but place great value on a stable network for partners. In the fewest cases, you can cover the entire value chain alone. You need strong and reliable partners at your side who work with you to drive the business forward. Start building your own ecosystem around your company. For example, you can use suppliers, producers, sales organizations, technology partners, and so on. Together, you can boost your success. The search for new partners, the management of the existing partners, and the repudiation of unprofitable partners should be one of the central tasks in Business Development.

1.10   Crisis as Opportunity

Crises present companies with major challenges. They affect customers' buying behavior, market conditions shift, supply chains collapse, and raw materials become scarce or more expensive.

In recent decades alone, there have been repeated major national and international crises, some of which have changed entire markets overnight. In the late 1990s and early 2000s, the New Economy plunged into a recession known as the dotcom crisis. Overnight, new digital companies around the world lost all their value, and deep distrust was directed at all digital trends. Then in 2007, the real estate bubble burst in the U.S., and overnight global financial markets convulsed, sending entire banks into bankruptcy. The Corona crisis certainly has a special status because, on the one hand, it affected every country worldwide and, on the other, all industries, and the effects are still not foreseeable. The effects of the Ukraine war also cannot yet be assessed (as of May 2022).

In addition to these "classical" crises, disruptive innovations can also cause crises. Modern streaming services for music and film are one example. Due to the paradigm shift from owning a medium to using a service "on demand", on the one hand, the sales figures of the media industry dropped rapidly and on the other hand, the classic media such as radio and TV are experiencing massive drops in listeners and viewers.

Crises have losers, but there are also always winners and companies that come through a crisis well or even strengthened. For example, crises often produce new companies that have adapted precisely to the new challenges and offer pinpoint solutions. This can lead to rapid corporate growth. However, it also carries the risk that customers' needs will change again after the crisis has subsided and there will no longer be a need for the solution. In this way, very specifically oriented companies can become redundant after a crisis and disappear from the market again.

In order to get through a crisis successfully as a company, the new market situation must be assessed and analyzed promptly. Then, offerings must be adapted so that they continue to be relevant under the changing circumstances. To believe that a company can successfully navigate through a crisis without making appropriate adjustments is very dangerous. Large companies with a broad customer and offering base can, with luck, get through a crisis well without adapting. However, this always carries the risk that the crisis will bring new competitors who have adapted optimally to the new situation and overtake traditional companies. Small companies often cannot afford to do this.

The Swiss writer Max Frisch said, "Crisis is a productive condition. You just have to take away the taint of disaster from it." Companies that have already implemented Business Development and an intact culture of innovation in the company find it much easier to flexibly align the company to the new circumstances in a crisis. After all, recognizing new customer requirements and consistently aligning the company's offerings with the market is the central task of Business Development.

Every crisis is therefore also an opportunity. An opportunity to put the company and its products and services to the test, to remove portfolio elements that are no longer in demand, and to develop and market new offerings that are currently in demand. With the help of targeted Business Development, a company can also completely reinvent itself in a crisis and emerge stronger from the crisis. However, Business Development is no guarantee that a company will successfully navigate through a crisis. Too many factors play a role that is beyond the company's direct control. However, it has been shown that companies that can adapt to changing requirements in an agile and timely manner are more resilient and more likely to navigate successfully through a crisis. Thus, Business Development can be the key to successfully navigating a crisis.

After the basics and prerequisites for successful Business Development have been explained in this chapter, the following chapters go into more detail on the individual areas of Business Development and help you to better understand and successfully implement them in your company.

Conclusion for Daily Business

- Business Development helps you succeed in ever-changing markets.
- Business Development, with its market observation, product development, portfolio, and partner management, performs many important tasks that help you align your products to the demands of the customer.
- Plan the goal of Business Development accurately and measure success.
- Incorporate the lean approach and accelerate your Business Development.
- Establish roundtables or a Business Development Board for regular exchange, communication, and information of all stakeholders.
- Constantly inform all employees about important changes in your company, the products, and services, and pay attention to successful change management if major changes occur.

- Remember that we live in VUCA times and go new ways.
- Use Ambidextry: Optimize your current business and develop new business at the same time.
- Work agile and break through rigid processes and structures.
- Create a corporate culture that is flexible and ready for change.
- A crisis can also be an opportunity. Use it to adapt your business to new customer needs and market conditions.

Business Development

Abstract

After describing the tasks of Business Development in the introduction, the individual dimensions of Business Development will be explained in detail below. It is not just a task. Business Development can also be seen as a role. A person who fulfills this role is also referred to as a Business Development Manager. The main features of a Business Development Manager are described below (see Sect. 2.2). At the same time, Business Development is also an organizational unit that has to be embedded in the structure of a company. Central and decentralized structures are possible here (see Sect. 2.4). Finally, Business Development can also be conceived as a process that prescribes a structure in the performance of tasks (see Sect. 2.5).

2.1   Mindset, Skillset, and Toolset

Business Development is a multidisciplinary task. It combines tasks from different areas of the company and requires a good overview of the industry as well as a deep understanding of the target customers and their needs. In order to be able to implement the task as a Business Development manager, three basic conditions must be met (see Fig. 2.1):

- *Mindset:* You are curious, open-minded, and adaptable. You have a positive attitude toward innovation and change. You have an agile mindset. You are able to learn and criticize and always question the status quo in order to permanently develop the company further.
- *Skillset:* You actively use your knowledge and experience and are committed to lifelong learning to always have needed skills and relevant expertise.
- *Toolset:* You know the relevant processes, methods, and tools and can use them safely depending on the situation.

© Springer Fachmedien Wiesbaden GmbH, part of Springer Nature 2023
A. Kohne, *Business Development*,
https://doi.org/10.1007/978-3-658-38844-7_2

Fig. 2.1 Correlation of
Business Development and
Mindset, Skillset, and Toolset

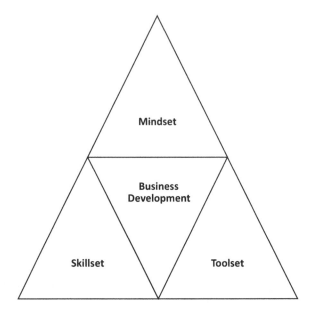

In the following, the role of Business Development and the most important skills are explained. In addition, all relevant processes, methods and tools are explained in detail in the further course.

2.2   Role

The simplest definition of a Business Development Manager is the entrepreneur in the company. He is responsible for assessing the existence of the existing product and service portfolio, evaluating it for further validity based on market changes, optimizing it for customer needs, and, if necessary, removing unnecessary items. For this purpose, the current status quo must constantly be questioned and challenged. That is why a Business Development Manager has to have sound knowledge in many areas. On the one hand, of course, profound, industry-specific knowledge has to be included in the role, but on the other hand, there should also be soft skills, such as communication and reflecting capability, as well as feedback capability. As a rule, a Business Development Manager will have a lot of customer contact in order to be permanently close to the target market. Furthermore, he must be able to communicate internally at "C level", meaning at the highest level of management. Furthermore, he should be open, enthusiastic, and motivating but always focused and goal-oriented. In addition, very good time management is needed. With all these features, blind actionism cannot arise. Otherwise, there is too much unrest in the running business and thus no help for it.

This type of personality structure is also called T-shape (see [12]). This term is to be understood literally. A successful person should be structured as the letter "T". The big pillar stands for profound, well-founded expertise. The two bars to the left and to the right overlap broad knowledge areas and their thematic borders, as well as the soft skills already described. Especially soft skills are becoming increasingly important as Business Development Manager must be able to exchange information with colleagues at different levels in the company. He also constantly exchanges ideas with customers and partners and needs to understand what motivates them and what their problems and challenges are. Furthermore, he often appears as a mediator and problem solver. Here, a high emotional intelligence (EQ) is needed, since interpersonal communication is central (see [15]). This combination of different personality structures and knowledge areas forms the basis for a successful Business Development Manager.

As Business Development is interdisciplinary, it can also be described as a modern decathlon in business life. The jobs in Business Development are often given to experienced sales or marketing staff. They already have experience with the respective products and services, often have customer contact, and are mostly well connected in the company. Often Business Development is given as an additional task on top of existing tasks. It is not advisable to do this because day-to-day business and potential pressure to reach goals do not leave any time to conscientiously undertake the tasks of a Business Development Manager. However, this decision also depends on the size of the company. Furthermore, engineers and product managers are also good candidates. They also bring important features to the role, but may need to be trained in financial and sales activities.

The features described so far show that Business Development is not an entry-level job. On the other hand, it is no job that can be learned in a normal training course. There are now first-degree programs that go in a similar direction. However, they only make sense for a part-time job, although the theories and methods of Business Development can be imparted to such a course, but the specific industry know-how is of course completely lacking.

When filling the Business Development Team, you should pay attention to the fact that you have a good mix and you want to select internal employees in combination with some people experienced in Business Development. That way, you ensure that the technical know-how and the knowledge about your company, your products, and services, your internal processes, and contacts are covered, and at the same time, you have specialist knowledge in the area of Business Development. This is of course only a solution for larger companies. If you want to establish Business Development in a smaller company, it is sometimes sufficient to take an experienced employee with a sales and technical background as a base and to offer him a corresponding training. The team can then grow as needed.

2.3   Role Profile

Below is an example role profile of an ideal Business Development Manager. It shows how diverse the requirements are. It also shows that Business Development requires a lot of industry knowledge combined with many soft skills. Thus, it should be clear that Business Development Manager is not an entry-level job, but is often staffed by experienced people in engineering, sales, and marketing.

The list is of course idealizing and not complete. In addition, the specific requirements for a Business Development manager may vary from company to company and from industry to industry.

Role Profile of a Business Development Manager

- Economics degree with a focus on marketing / sales, Business Development / computer science / business administration, or a comparable degree.
- At least three years of relevant job experience in the target industry.
- International experience.
- Sound knowledge of business management, processes, and controlling.
- Very good English as well as at least one other foreign language (often French, Spanish, German, Russian, or Chinese).
- Willingness to take on the project and result responsibility.
- Well-founded analytical and strategic thinking.
- High problem-solving competence and "can-do mentality".
- Ability to structure complex tasks professionally.
- Outstanding communication skills and sensitivity to customers.
- Sales personality.
- Team Player.
- Sovereign appearance on all hierarchical levels.
- Willingness to travel.
- Sales thinking and way of working.
- Strategic thinking.
- Experience in a management consultancy.
- Experience in project management (e.g., PRINCE-2, PMP, or IPMA).
- Ability to identify new business opportunities.
- Excellent analytical skills and solution-oriented thinking.
- Experiences with agile development methods (e.g., Scrum).
- Lean start-up mentality.
- High personal initiative.
- Responsibility and quality awareness.
- High flexibility.

- Empathic and customer-oriented problem solver.
- Experienced work with MS Office, especially PowerPoint and Excel.

2.4   Organizational Unit

After describing the tasks, role, and role profile of a Business Development Manager in the previous chapters, this chapter discusses the organizational structure. The question arises as to how Business Development can be integrated into the existing company structure. The concrete implementation is of course different from company to company and depends not least on the size and structure of the company. Basically, there are two possibilities of integration:

1. *Centralized:* This option creates a new organizational unit for Business Development purposes. In it, all employees work under a supervisor. As it is a strategically important entity, it is often placed directly under the management or board. The employees in this team can then be assigned to specific subject areas in the specialist departments, or take over changing tasks and projects. Typically, however, the employees' know-how is more or less linked to specific topics.
2. *Decentralized:* There is no dedicated team for this option, but the Business Development Managers work in the respective organizational unit to help them develop the business. Often directly under the head of each unit. This has the advantage that mostly employees from the respective environment are selected for this task. Thus, they know the products, tasks, processes, customers, and internal contact persons. However, it should be noted that the employees still comply with the centrally defined process. In order to avoid deviations and duplication, to make use of synergies, and to strengthen the communication between the individual Business Development Managers, at least a regular, central meeting should be planned to coordinate activities and to optimize the processes in which all relevant employees exchange views (see Sect. 2.5.11 (Lessons Learned) and Sect. 2.5.12 (Continuous Improvement Process)).

But before deciding on one of the two variants, a few basic topics should be decided first:

- *Goals:* In the beginning, you should clearly and in writing formulate the goals that Business Development pursues. This formulation may be passed to the new department or employee after approval by management as a concrete work assignment. Make sure that the goals are complete and specifically formulated. Make sure that the goals are formulated in concrete terms. It has proven to be an advantage to define goals using the so-called "SMART" procedure. SMART stands for the following(see [11]):
  - *S—Specific:* Goals must be very concrete and clearly defined.

- **M—*Measurable:*** Achieving the goals must be measured against previously uniquely defined criteria and metrics.
- **A—*Accepted:*** The defined goals must be agreed upon and accepted by all sides. They are the basis for collaboration.
- **R—*Realistic:*** The goals must be achievable. It is important to ensure that the goals are nevertheless demanding.
- **T—*Time-bound:*** The goals must be clearly scheduled. That is, each goal and subgoal has a clear start and end point.

Think carefully about what goal you want to achieve with the introduction of Business Development. This is the only way to ensure that not just anything is done, but to specifically develop new portfolio elements and / or evolve existing ones. Should new markets be opened up? New customer segments to be integrated? Should the portfolio or individual elements be internationalized?

- ***Rights:*** It is very important to be aware of the rights of such a department or person before launching Business Development. The position of Business Development can either be made very strong and extensive or as a pure idea generator. It has to be clarified exactly how Business Development interacts with the individual areas and persons of the company and to what degree they have the right to participate. What can be directly influenced, for example? Which decisions can be made alone? What decisions must be made in management?

  Furthermore, it has to be clarified exactly what the communication and cooperation with the partners look like. How is the company externally represented? May new partner contracts be concluded from Business Development, or must this be decided centrally? This is followed by M & A (Mergers and Acquisitions) (see Sect. 4.5). Is it a Business Development task to seek out possible acquisition targets, make contact, and possibly even negotiate? Is this strategically intended, or is it already being adopted by another department?

  The last point concerns the customer interface. How should Business Development occur to customers? Should Business Development employees also work as pre-sales consultants? Can Business Development independently acquire new customers or projects, or do sales always have to be included?

- ***Responsibilities:*** This topic overlaps strongly with the previous one. However, exact responsibilities for Business Development should be specified in advance. These can then be provided with appropriate rights. Possible responsibilities (besides the actual Business Development) of Business Development could be the following:

  1. Market monitoring.
  2. Partner management.
  3. Pre-Sales-Consulting.
  4. Sales-Enablement.
  5. Mergers and Acquisitions.
  6. Portfolio management.

7. Product management.
8. Controlling support.
9. Marketing support.

This list must be customized by each company. But it gives a good overview of the range of possible responsibilities. The individual points will be presented in-depth in the course of this book.

No matter which organizational implementation you decide on in your company: Tell each Business Development Manager the following: "There is only one supervisor: the market".

2.5 Process

After the tasks, the role and the organizational implementation possibilities of Business Development have been explained in the last chapters, and the actual process is presented in detail in the following. Please note that this is a prototypical process that needs to be adapted to each company's specific needs. Furthermore, not all phases of the process need to be strictly handled, parts may (sometimes) be eliminated, or new parts or whole phases added.

The Business Development process is shown graphically in Fig. 2.2. It begins by defining the goal of the respective Business Development activity. If a measurable goal is determined, the actual process can be started. Now you can begin to gather ideas that may be ingrained in product ideas or enhancements (see Sect. 2.5.1). Once the first valid ideas have been found, a project plan can be set up for the further course of the process (see Sect. 2.5.2). Following this, the underlying Business Model (see Sect. 2.5.3) followed by a Concrete Business Plan (see Sect. 2.5.4) is prepared and discussed with management. After release by the management, the development phase can be started (see Sect. 2.5.6). At first, a prototype should be created at an early stage (see Sect. 2.5.5). This helps to better understand the product, to discuss it early with customers, and to integrate feedback into the further process. This is followed by an exhaustive test phase (see Sect. 2.5.7). The product should be extensively tested internally, with customers and partners. Also, the collected feedback should again improve the product. If all tests are completed, the realization phase can be started (see Sect. 2.5.8). Here, the actual product is created, produced, operated, configured, offered, and sold (depending on the type of product or service). Completing the Business Development Process will be a Lessons Learned Phase, in which you will re-direct the whole process to get better each time you pass (see Sect. 2.5.11). In addition, the entire process is enhanced by (internal and maybe external) communication measures (see Sect. 2.5.9), and all process steps, (sub-) results, and decisions are documented in writing (see Sect. 2.5.10). Of course, a justified termination of the process is also possible at any time. Frequently, loops also occur between the individual process steps, since individual steps require several iterations in order to provide an optimal result.

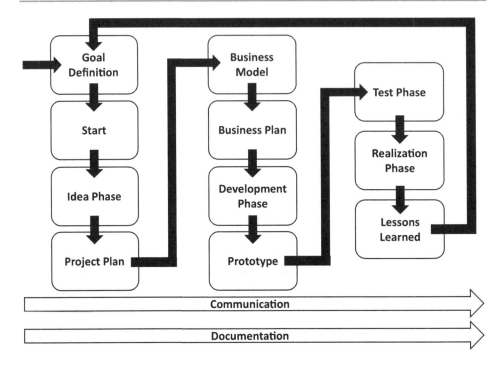

Fig. 2.2 The prototypical Business Development process

Having reviewed the actual process, you'll need to think about a few things before implementing it in your organization. First, you should be absolutely clear on how and, above all, who can start the process. Where do the proposals for development come from? Does the management specify topics? Are new topics being developed exclusively in Business Development? Is it possible for each employee to submit suggestions for improvement at a central point (this would require a corresponding process to be defined and a correspondingly open culture prevailing in the company)? Do you come up with ideas from production, sales, or marketing? Or is it perhaps a mixture of several possibilities?

When is the process completed? And above all, where are defined points in your process that can be taken as a central decision to abort or continue a project? A (for example, economically) reasoned process termination should be possible at all times so as not to waste valuable resources.

When designing and implementing the process in your company, be aware that it is as lightweight as possible. Bear in mind that Business Development should help your company act faster and more agile on the market and adapt quickly to changing market conditions. In addition, the process must be lightweight, agile, and easily adaptable to changing circumstances.

The following chapters describe the individual phases of the Business Development Process in detail.

2.5.1 Idea Phase

The Business Development Process starts with the idea phase. But before it can start, the goal must first be defined quite concretely. Do you want to improve, expand, update, or even internationalize an existing product or service, or do you want to create a completely new product?

In the first case, this may mean that you need to think about how to improve the product. Can you refine it? Here is often spoken of a so-called value-add. Can the existing product be upgraded in any way? Can you make it better, faster, or cheaper? Here, the basis is the existing product. In the second case, you start from zero, so to speak. You have to develop a completely new idea. The basis of all your considerations should always be the expectation of your customers. What does the customer expect from you? How does your product or service help solve a customer problem? How can you help him achieve his goals?

That's why they should first be aware of where your customer's bottleneck lies. What depresses him, and where and how can you position yourself as the best possible problem solver for your customer? In order to approach these and other questions, you should familiarize yourself with the topic Bottleneck-concentrated Strategy[1]. The strategy assumes that it is worthwhile to focus on and build on its strengths, and then, after a profound analysis of the customer's bottleneck, develop a solution that suits precisely that need in a very clear way and a clearly outlined customer segment. Often, such solutions can be developed for niche markets. The goal is to gain market leadership in a given segment through absolute focus and constant optimization.

But even if you target your products and services to a broader or even a mass market, it is worthwhile to carry out a bottleneck analysis. This is best when you talk a lot and often with your clients and your colleagues who are in charge of the customers, in order to permanently learn what moves their customers. This may be the source of market currents that you can use.

If your job is to develop a new product, you should make a profound market analysis ahead of time. Clarify where areas are in need. But on the other hand, also clarify whether there are already products in the market that cover this need (at least in parts). If so, consider whether this market is still of interest to you, or whether you want to seek something else. If you decide on this market, you must decide whether you want to enter the so-called Me-Too business. In doing so, you also develop a solution that is similar to the one already existing. How far you want to do this is up to you. In extreme cases, when trying to offer an exact

---

[1] The Bottleneck-concentrated Strategy (from the German "Engpass-konzentrierte Strategie (EKS)") was developed in 1970 by Wolfgang Mewes. It is protected by copyright and all rights are owned by Malik Management Zentrum St. Gallen AG.

copy of an existing product, we talk about so-called Copy-Cats. Here, you should make sure that products are mostly protected by copyright.

The decision between an already occupied market and a new one is often referred to as "Red Ocean vs. Blue Ocean". The underlying Blue Ocean strategy states that it is better for lasting business success to create a new market or to open up a completely new market with a modified or completely new product innovation (see [24]). This has several advantages: Since it is a new market with a new product, there is still no competition. Thus, you have an easy game in the acquisition and can achieve a high sales value for lack of alternatives, which can quickly recoup the development costs possibly incurred. If, on the other hand, you enter a fully developed market with a new product, then you are entering shark pools of competitors that may have been successful in the market for a long time and have shared the entire market share among themselves. Hence the name: (blood) Red Ocean. So, there is a sheer cut-throat market, in which (assuming a really good product) you have to be very aggressive, and you may have to work (especially at the beginning) with very low selling prices to gain market share. An often quoted example of an optimal Blue Ocean strategy is the Nintendo Wii game console.

Example

The market of game consoles is a maximally developed one, which is basically occupied by three manufacturers Nintendo, Sony (Playstation), and Microsoft (XBox). At a time when Sony and Microsoft were targeting the intensive player market, Nintendo's Wii entered the completely unoccupied market of casual gamers and families with young children. Nintendo developed a completely new console, which was easy to use with an innovative gesture control and, in contrast to the other consoles, was also cheaper, since no high-end hardware was used. The launch was a complete success, and Nintendo made money from the first console, as they did not subsidize their console, unlike Sony and Microsoft, to recoup the hardware costs afterward by selling games and other online services. So Nintendo was fully committed to a Blue Ocean strategy and had the desired success. ◄

To reposition a product (or your entire portfolio) in the direction of a Blue Ocean strategy, four approaches have emerged as follows (see [24]):

1. *Eliminate:* Which parts, functions, extensions, and features of your offer can you omit? What is the market perhaps no longer in demand? What do your customers never use? Which new market requirements are no longer covered in the previous constellation?
2. *Reduce:* What features and functions can be reduced? How can costs be saved in production, storage, and distribution?
3. *Upgrading:* What features and functions of your product need to be improved or rebuilt? What requirements does your target market have? How can you help by improving? How does this create a unique selling proposition?

4. *Create:* What do you need to rebuild to address your target market? Do you need to create a complete new product or service? Is it enough to provide a product through additional and innovative services? What do your customers really need? What does the competition not (yet) offer?

After the Idea Phase has been presented in detail in this chapter, I would like to introduce a few useful tools for generating ideas here. Of course, only a few are presented here. Further, the field of creativity techniques is much larger. If you are looking for more information about this area, you will quickly find it on the Internet. Furthermore, there is a lot of literature on the subject. Here is a small selection:

- *Brainstorming:* Brainstorming is one of the best-known methods for developing new ideas (see [47]). It can be done alone or in a group. But there are some basic rules in brainstorming that not all know. In order to go through the process properly, it is very important to pay close attention to the rules. Whether you work alone or in a group: Allow all thoughts and ideas. Do not comment on or criticize any idea, no matter how absurd it sounds at this moment. Encourage yourself or your colleagues to build on existing ideas and develop them further. This can quickly create certain group dynamics. Continue to document every idea. It is best if you write them down big and legible in a central location, so that all ideas can be seen at any time. When writing down, do not worry about grouping or prioritization. At this point, all ideas are equivalent. Give yourself or the group a clear timeline, for example, half an hour, and then finish the process afterward without strangling ideas. Only in the next step will the collected ideas be evaluated and structured. For this purpose, you can use a Mind Map for example.
- *Mind Mapping:* In Mind Mapping, an idea or topic is written in the middle of a large piece of paper (see [9]). For example, this could be a generic term for your new idea that you've already worked on with the help of brainstorming. It is best to draw a circle around the term or underline it so that it is clearly recognizable. In the next step, you try to assign generic terms to the collected ideas. These generic terms, grouping terms, or clusters are written down next and connect the new term to the central term using a line. From there, you can branch out any further and thus concretize the idea piece by piece and add details. A new generic term then gets a direct connection to the central term again. The result is an orderly network, which graphically presents your idea. It has also been found that it is useful not only to use text on a mind map, but also to work with pictures, graphics, or small pictograms. This makes the individual ideas more striking and better remembered.

  To work more flexibly with this tool, it is advisable to use a computer program to create the Mind Map. There are various systems from free-open source versions to multi-user enterprise software. Such programs help you to structure your mind map, and you can arrange your points automatically and you can move entire parts of the diagram with a mouse click, in order to restructure the Mind Map. In addition, the result can be easily saved and sent, for example, by e-mail to all involved.

- **Design Thinking:** Design Thinking has become very popular in recent years. Large companies such as Google and BMW use this method. Unlike many other creative methods, design thinking always begins with the customers in mind. The entire method is centered on an (imaginary) customer, moving from its needs and perceptions toward an idea. Design Thinking consists of three elements, which are presented in the following (see [35]). The basis of cooperation are the following rules:

1. Be visual.
2. One conversation at a time.
3. Encourage wild ideas.
4. Defer judgment.
5. Go for quantity.
6. Stay on topic.
7. Build on the ideas of others.

1. **Process:** The actual Design Thinking process is divided into six iterative steps that are followed one after the other. At the same time, it is quite possible and desirable for some phases to be run through several times in order to provide feedback as quickly as possible and to refine the idea step by step. In the following, the six steps are presented:

   a. **Understand:** The first step opens up the problem area and helps all participants to understand the starting situation. It describes what the real problem is, how the customer (group) is set together, and how they may be able to solve the problem today.

   b. **Observe:** The second step should be used to better understand the problem and the environment in field studies through observation or research and to map the status quo in the best possible way.

   c. **Define perspective:** After that, the findings are projected onto a prototypical user in the third step. This is done in the form of a so-called persona. This persona is given a name, age, gender, and a complete social background such as marital status, place of residence, circle of friends, and work environment. Once such a persona has been created, the problem is seen from the perspective of just that persona. Ask questions such as: How do I perceive the problem? When do I meet him? Have I found solutions for myself? With whom can I talk about the problem? How could a new solution help me to improve my situation? What would be improved by a new solution?

   d. **Find ideas:** Then, in the fourth step, start to find creative solutions to the problem. Everything is allowed in the first step. For example, here you can start brainstorming again. The resulting ideas can then be structured, for example, with the help of a mind map. Then find the best idea and continue to develop it.

e. ***Develop a prototype:*** A major advantage of Design Thinking is that prototypes are already being used at a very early stage. This is exactly what happens in the next step in phase five. Now try to model your idea from phase four using the materials provided. Be open and do not put too much emphasis on the look. It should be quickly created as a product that can be worked on plastically. Creating a prototype makes the idea more real. This helps immensely in the further discussion since the product is already tactile to experience. For example, if the idea is a service, you can paint flowcharts and interaction graphs. If it is software, you can also create a first prototype using paper. This is also called a paper GUI (see Sect. 2.5.5).

f. ***Test:*** In the sixth and final step, the prototype is tested. For this purpose, additional employees can be called in, or even better, real customers can be involved. If customers like what they see, you can ask customers for further wishes or improvements. Collect all feedback and include it in the prototypes. If the customer does not like your idea at all, you can reject the prototype at this point as quickly as you created it. This is the advantage of this fast method. From this step, you should branch back to one of the previous process steps. For example, this can mean rebuilding or reworking the prototype, or even getting you back to the drawing board completely. Use the speed of the process to quickly run your idea through multiple iterations and improve it every turn.

2. ***Multidisciplinary teams:*** In Design Thinking, great emphasis is placed on teams that are composed of as many areas as possible. Thus, it should be ensured that as many ideas as possible come together. Often people in such a process are engaged in marketing, development, production, and distribution. As a result, the attitude to the newly developed item is different. You may also involve people who have not previously been involved in such a project because they are not impacted by past experiences, thereby bringing creative ideas to the process.

3. ***Variable room concepts:*** When planning and implementing a Design Thinking Workshop, make sure that the room offers as many creative possibilities as possible. For this, it should be made big, bright, and open. There should be enough space for whiteboards, metaplan walls, and other drawing materials. Furthermore, you should provide tables on which materials are already available that can be used to create the prototypes. What you use here depends heavily on the desired end result. You can use paper, pens, plasticine, fabrics, Lego bricks, wood, or other materials. The entire work should be carried out during the process in small groups of about six people. Make sure that you can work while standing and that you can exchange ideas between different teams.

The whole process should be led and accompanied by an experienced moderator. This ensures that the process and the rules are kept. Furthermore, the moderator should specify timing presets for the individual steps. Here, the span may be between a few minutes and whole hours or even days per process step, depending on the complexity. Again, it is important that all results are documented. At best, all sub-groups will present their results to the whole group at the end. Thus, further discussions can be started immediately and, possibly, a ranking of the developed ideas can be created so that they can be further pursued according to prioritization.

- *Maker Thinking:* Another innovative approach to develop creative, new business models was designed by Martin Kiel on the think tank "the black frame".[2] In the Maker Thinking approach, unlike in Design Thinking, where ideas are first developed on paper and post-it, it is all about producing tangible results right from the start.

  Maker thinking is understood as an external impulse for internal innovation. In doing so, approaches from the innovation management are combined with the ideas of the maker scene (see [16]). The process is started by bringing in an external, multidisciplinary team of experts to a mixed internal team. The composition of this team is individual to each innovation project and can range from engineers, (interior or exterior) architects, and start-up consultants to IT and marketing professionals. It is recommended to involve five to seven specialists in the project.

  Maker Thinking can be subdivided into three consecutive phases. The first two phases are limited to six days each. The third phase usually takes three to six months. These phases proceed as described below:

1. *Innovation Camp:* The ideas for possible new business models and products are not developed in a conference room, but developed in excursions to customers, through cities, parks, and buildings. During this phase, new impressions of the customer's reality should be collected and new customer requirements made tangible on site. It is about an open discourse with the social present and an active experience of the current popular culture. According to the black frame, only by active engagement with the present can sustainable ideas be developed for the future. In this immersive approach, the company is supposed to reinvent itself from within, using new input from the real world as a template for new ideas. Despite the omnipresent digitization, the focus at the beginning should not be on an IT solution. For example, the idea of trying to do something with blockchain technology (just because it's trendy) is wrong. This choice of supporting IT should first be postponed and the actual product or business model should be developed with true customer value.

2. *Do Tank / Visioneering:* In the second phase, concrete ideas for a new product or business model are developed. Here, the approach differs from other approaches, where ideas are first developed and evaluated purely on paper, before a prototype may be developed at a later stage. Maker Thinking immediately develops prototypes. In this rapid prototyping, for example, 3D prints of future products, real shop fittings, and product populations or click dummies of software products and apps can

---

[2] the black frame., www.theblackframe.com.

be developed. This is how the new products can be experienced immediately. In addition, everything is already being prepared to turn the new business model into a real business. New marketing pages, logos, and brand claims can be created, social media channels prepared, and personnel planning started. In addition, everything is prepared for a smooth IT integration.

The prototype created in this way is already tested together with customers in this phase and accompanied by a predefined Innovation accounting. This measures and evaluates previously defined key performance indicators (KPIs). These may include traffic to a product page, trial sales, customer numbers in a new store, app downloads, and of course verbal and written customer feedback.

At the end of this phase, a complete product has been created and already tested and evaluated. This is then presented to the management, which has to decide whether the product or the new business model should be turned into reality. Since this approach is quite radical and, above all, fast, top management must be involved right from the start and the process must be wanted and supported.

If the management decides positively at this point, everything has already been handed over to the extent that the new concept can be implemented immediately.

3. **Launch Pad:** The real implementation then takes place in the third phase. In doing so, the previously developed results are taken as the basis for the new solution. Mostly something completely new arises at this point, which is often (at first) implemented in a newly founded company or product area. In order to maintain the speed that was built up in the development phase, a lean start-up approach is chosen here (see Sect. 1.8). Thus, literally, the switch can be pushed and the new business model comes to life. Innovation accounting should continue to be used during this phase to provide management with permanent information about the performance of the new company or product.

With the help of Maker Thinking and the use of an interdisciplinary team, new business models can be developed, tested, and put into live use very quickly.

- **Destroy our Business:** This method is very radical, but can produce very creative ideas. In the Destroy your Business method, you group together a group of approximately six people with a moderator. It is best to create a calm atmosphere outside normal everyday life. The moderator briefly explains the rules of the game at the beginning and then guides the participants through the process on the basis of specific questions. The participants should spend approximately two hours together and decide who or what could endanger your company. It is considered together how the company or a specific product or service could be threatened by a competitor or even made superfluous. For example, the moderator can ask the following questions:
  - How could a high-end business model or a small start-up copy or reform your classic business model?
  - How would the competition make your business model better?

- Is there a business model that could make your complete business obsolete?
- What would the product or the business model look like?
- How could your competitor take away your customers?
- Why would a customer switch to a competitor?
- How would your competitor present your product?
- How do the competitive pricing structures look like?

Once at least one threat scenario has been developed and documented based on these questions, the next step is to start deducing the bottom line for the business and developing ideas for a new business model, product, or service. These ideas can then be reintegrated into the Business Development process.

Example

Probably the most famous example of the successful use of the Destroy your Business method is Amazon. The Internet retailer grew up selling classic books. Of course, Amazon is now selling everything, but at the beginning, the company focused on the online book trade. In the early 2000s, several Amazon employees and managers teamed up to use the Destroy your Business method to modernize their business. As part of the process, it was recognized that electronic books are increasingly on the rise. First traders already sold the so-called e-books and the market (especially the US market) grew rapidly. As a result, Amazon saw its classic bookstore business in danger and wondered how a new e-book company would operate. The solution is as simple as it is ingenious: A cheap e-book reader (Amazon Kindle) was developed, which could only be filled with books from the Amazon shop. At the same time, corresponding contracts were signed with e-book publishers, so that the book offer was very large from the beginning. Amazon has been able to penetrate the market very quickly and bind many customers worldwide. ◄

- *Design Sprint:* In the area of digital business models and products (for example, software, smartphone, table apps, or cloud-based services), another creative method has gained acceptance in recent years. The method was developed by Google and is called Design Sprint. It is designed to produce a completely new business model including a finished prototype within five days.
  The procedure is structured on a daily basis and can be summarized as follows (see: [2]):
  - *First day: Introduction* The first day is used so that the interdisciplinary team with employees from different departments and areas get to know each other and current problems and challenges are presented.
  - *Second day: Sketch* On the second day, based on the presented challenges, initial solutions are developed and sketches for possible products are developed in small groups.

- *Third day: Decide* The previously prepared idea sketches will be presented to a jury on the second day. This should be filled with decision makers, since the ideas developed later become real products. This is the only way to ensure that resources (money and people) are available for implementation after the Design Sprint and that the management supports the idea. Once all the ideas have been presented, the best approach will be selected by the panel.
- *Fourth day: Prototype* On the fourth day, the idea that won the day before is implemented in the first working prototype. All of the team members work together on the implementation and develop an executable software that already implements basic functions.
- *Fifth day: Validate* The last day is used to test the prototype. For this purpose, potential target customers or employees who are not involved in the Design Sprint can be used to gain initial reactions to the new product and to ask for feedback and suggestions for improvement.

This procedure is fast and already delivers a prototype within just one working week. The last day's customer feedback can then be used to decide whether the prototype should evolve into a product, whether the product should not bring the desired benefit, or should be reconsidered fundamentally. In the best case, it was possible to develop a viable new business model, including a first implementation, in only one week, which then can be developed into a full product in the next step. In the worst case, only five days were invested and the company is at least one experience richer. Anyway, the feedback should be included in the next Design Sprint. This way, the quality of the Design Sprints can be increased every time.

- *Hackathons:* Another way to quickly develop and test creative ideas are Hackathons (cf. [25]). The word Hackathon consists of the words "to hack" (meaning to program) and "marathon". A Hackathon is basically organized like a contest in which either completely free or under specification of a technology or a topic, new ideas, programs, services, or mobile apps are developed. Several teams work together over a defined period of time, work out the basic ideas, and then develop a first, executable prototype in the given time, which is then presented to a jury at the end.

Hackathons have become very popular in recent years and are appreciated by industry and government alike. It should be noted that Hackathons can only be used to test and develop IT-based solutions.

Hackathons can be carried out internally in a company and with their own personnel or with external persons. The teams should be as heterogeneous as possible so that different skills and competencies can be used.

A Hackathon usually lasts two to three days, during which work is often very intensive around the clock. At fixed times, the jury must be presented with intermediate results. These are, for example, the business model, a technical planning, and a schedule of the further procedure.

At the end of a Hackathon, all participants come together and present the results to the jury and the other participants. The jury then decides on the win according to a predetermined list of criteria. Prizes often include cash or prizes awarded by the employer or sponsors. Hackathons can have different goals. The following are the three most important ones:

1. *Developing New Business Models* Especially in the context of digitization, companies need new business models that either create a whole new business or are an evolution of the existing business model. As part of a Hackathon, creative ideas can be quickly developed and tested. That is why it is a good idea to take part in the competition with external participants and to involve only a few of your own employees. This ensures that participants can think more freely and are not caught within the limitations of a company's day-to-day business.

2. *Try New Technologies* Hackathons can also be used to quickly try out new IT technologies. Whether it is integrating cloud services or using a mobile app, for example. Within the framework of a competition, new ideas and technological innovations can be examined quickly and without much financial outlay on their possible uses for their own company.

3. *Find New Staff* Another way to use Hackathons, which has recently become very popular in the shortage of skilled workers, is to use the competition to quickly find highly qualified candidates, to check them for technical and social skills in the context of the competition, and to offer them a job directly afterward.

• *The magic question:* The magic question is the simple question: "What if…?". Here you can add a corresponding part depending on your respective destination. For example: "What if our products were a bestseller in Europe, too?", "What if we had no budget worries?", "What if we were the market leader overnight?", or better still: "What if tomorrow everything was going to be perfect?". Such questions open a wide space, which is very positively occupied. Thus, such questions help to ignore the past difficulties and problems and stimulate completely free thinking about a given topic. Keep in mind that just like brainstorming, you allow all answers. Document everything again and encourage your colleagues to broaden the question, perhaps to gather more ideas. After a predetermined period of time, the ideas are then reviewed, evaluated, and looked at, whether or not conclusions can be drawn from this for the actual situation.

If you have developed a concrete idea, you can put it to a real stress test. For that a "Kill or Thrill" discussion is appropriate. It introduces the idea to a group of people (including people who were not involved in the development of the idea) and then they search for reasons why you should refuse to implement that idea for 20 min. Again, allow all replies and write them down. Collect all feedback without criticism. Thereafter, together they will seek reasons for 20 min that will make the idea a success. Again, allow all answers. Then summarize all the answers and think about how the answers could advance your idea. Correct the idea accordingly or discard it at this time, when the negative points outweigh or absolute no-go arguments were found. This is no problem. You have lost nothing at this time. But you have gained experience. Asked about his years of failing to invent the light bulb, Thomas Edison replied, "I have not failed, I know more than 1000 ways of not constructing a light bulb".

After you have produced at least one valid idea in this phase, it's time to put it into more concrete terms. If you have several valid ideas, they must be evaluated in detail and then the idea with the highest probability of success is selected. Possibly, the ideas won are so different that it would be worthwhile to pursue several more. The decision is up to the management in this case.

Once the final idea has been selected, you should not worry too much about sorting it into your portfolio at this point in the process. Rather, keep thinking freely and without the limitations of your previous business. This ensures that the idea can continue to grow without being limited by everyday life. However, at a later stage (when the innovation process is complete), you will need to clarify how you want to incorporate the new product into your portfolio. Does the product even fit into your existing portfolio? Do you thereby cannibalize other products / areas / markets / partners? Does the product fit your image? If you have answered no to some of these questions and still want to bring the product to market, it pays to think about whether you might want to start a new business for marketing or start a joint venture with a partner. This is especially useful for products that stand far outside the existing portfolio.

In addition to the internal development of innovations, an approach has become established in recent years in which customers are directly involved in the idea phase. This method, known as "co-creation", is described next.

2.5.1.1 Co-creation

In recent years, there has been a clear shift from a "product-centric" to a "customer-centric" approach. Until now, the product (or service) was at the center of companies. Everything revolved around development, production, marketing, and sales. Today, the customer is at the center. Because without customers, all other actions are superfluous. It's about understanding the customer and solving his problems.

Business Development should be close to the customer and his problems. Instruments from market research and market observation are classically used for this purpose. It has been shown that it can also be a very good idea to involve customers directly in the development process. This approach is known as Co-creation. In this case, the ideas of the customers are used directly and the innovative potential of the customer base is leveraged.

There are no specific rules when it comes to implementing co-creation. For example, you can invite your customers to open innovation discussions and talk about new ideas at a round table. Furthermore, you can call on your customers to submit new and innovative ideas. This approach is often carried out as an idea competition with corresponding prizes.

In addition to offline implementation, it is also possible to use co-creation processes online. This is referred to as crowdsourcing. The word is made up of the two words crowd and outsourcing (for example, the outsourcing of IT operations to a service provider). With the help of social media, crowdsourcing campaigns can be carried out quickly and easily, as you are already connected to your target customers via your company profiles and can directly place a corresponding call on the respective platforms.

Large sporting goods manufacturers have often used this tool to develop new designs for T-shirts or shoes in small creative competitions. Users could create or upload their own designs via an online platform and the community was then allowed to vote for the individual designs. In this way, manufacturers were able to solve more than one problem at a time, as they not only received attractive new designs, they also came into a very close exchange with their target customers, tied them even more closely to the company, and at the same time received direct feedback on potential new products. In this way, they could be sure that the production of the new products with the winning designs would find great sales. This can be secured, for example, with an integrated pre-order process.

For all the advantages, it should also be pointed out that co-creation processes also entail possible disadvantages or risks. For example, open discussion at a very early stage of development can provide competitors with important information about potentially unprotected products. Furthermore, manipulation can easily occur on the Internet. For example, online platforms can be attacked or abused by coordinated protests.

However, open idea competitions can also be distorted by participants who are just making fun. A well-known example comes from 2011. The German dishwashing liquid company Pril, which belongs to the Henkel Group, invited its customers to participate in an online design competition. Customers were able to develop new designs for the dishwashing liquid bottle on a special platform or upload their own designs. Among many serious and creative entries, one participant uploaded a picture of a hand-drawn chicken underneath which it read, "Tastes delicious like chicken!" This design went viral on social media overnight and was "liked" and shared thousands of times. A viral phenomenon was created. As a result, the design ended up in first place by a wide margin, as people all over the Internet were calling to vote for it. Nevertheless, the winning design was not printed at that time, because after the user evaluation there was still an internal jury that selected the final winning design from the ten best designs (cf. [6]).

It is therefore very important to plan co-creation processes precisely and to back them up with very clearly communicated and enforced rules. If you stick to them, you can use co-creation and crowdsourcing to harness the innovative power of your customers for your benefit.

After you have successfully completed your idea phase (in-house or together with customers), it is time to create a concrete project plan.

2.5.2 Project Plan

The idea is now fixed. It is already concretized and now waiting to be worked out. For this purpose, it will now be guided step by step through the Business Development Process.

However, in order to carry out this procedure as specified, you must create a concrete project plan at this point (see [46]). The blueprint of the process serves as a template. You now have to think carefully about which people you need for the project, who are the key stakeholders, which skills will be needed for how long in the project, and so on. Of crucial importance is the estimation of the budget needed for development. Only when a concrete project plan and an estimate of the costs incurred have been created can it be decided at the management level whether an investment in this process is worthwhile.

When creating the project plan, the classic methods of project management are used. Since there are a variety of process models and each company has a preferred approach, which was certainly also customized, this topic will not be discussed at this point in the preparation of the project plan. Just make sure that a plan that is as concrete as possible, with appropriate milestones, persons in charge, and deadlines, is created and maintained permanently during the project. This is the responsibility of the project manager. This can but does not have to come from Business Development.

It is assumed below that there is a positive management decision regarding the proposed project. Of course, the process can also be stopped at this point. Then the idea phase would be started again.

2.5.3 Business Model

Your new product idea or product customization will help you to make a business break-through. You should successfully position and distribute the product to your target market. To do this, you must be clear about what exactly you want to sell and what your cost and revenue structures look like. Exactly this is summarized under the term Business Model. The Business Model describes all aspects of your product and the market in which you move.

In recent years, the so-called Business Model Canvas has been adopted for the development and description of the Business Model (see [33]). It is used by many large international companies, and especially by start-ups, to quickly and easily write down what your business looks like, where the added value is, how the product is created, and how it is distributed to customers. The advantage of the Business Model Canvas is that it is a very simple graphical method that is easy to learn and use. The canvas allows quick creation and customization of Business Models. This is very important, as your model will certainly be adapted and refined several times in the course of the Business Development Process.

The individual fields of the Business Model Canvas are described in the following, with the descriptions referring to Fig. 2.3:

1. *Value Propositions:* This is the key point and should be your starting point in creating your Canvas. In this field, you describe your value proposition. What does your product offer? What sets it apart from other products in the market? What makes it unique? What is your USP (Unique Selling Proposition or Unique Selling Point)? Which problem or

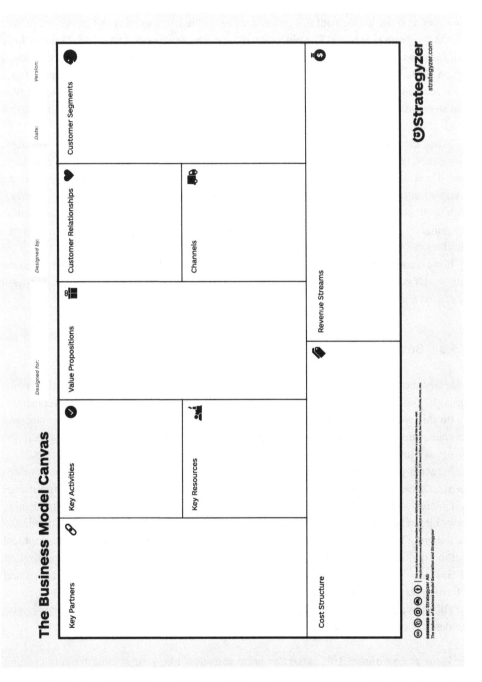

Fig. 2.3 The Business Model Canvas. (This graphic is provided by Strategyzer AG under the creative commons (cc) license (CCBY-SA3.0)

which challenge of the customer do you solve with the product? Be as specific as possible and present the most important features in a concrete and easy-to-understand way. Use a few technical languages as possible. Your product should be understood later by all your customers.

2. *Customer Segments:* In this section of the Canvas, you describe your target customers. You may have a customer segment. Maybe more than one. Clearly define these and explain the specific needs of each segment as accurately as possible. For this, you should use the results of market research (see Chap. 5).

3. *Customer Relationships:* Here you describe what your customer relationships look like. Do you sell your product directly? Do you have middlemen? If so, what do they look like? How do these dealers sell your product? Describe your sales structure as precisely as possible and show all sales levels.

4. *Channels:* The channels are the ways to connect with your customers. Do you use sales-people who visit the customer? Do you sell through an online store? Do you distribute your products through wholesalers or do you exhibit at trade fairs? Describe all relevant channels and what segments you are trying to reach. Remember that different customers have different communication preferences. Again, you can use the results of market research (see Chap. 5).

5. *Key Activities:* Here you should outline what your core activity is to create the product. Does it have to be produced in a factory? Do permanent developments and operational activities have to be carried out (for example software)? What are the core activities without which your product would not exist? Often here are the company secrets, because here the actual production is described, which makes your product unique.

6. *Key Resources:* In this field, you describe what your key resources are. Are these special employees with special know-how? Are these raw materials or prefabricated product groups of third-party suppliers? Describe exactly how your product is made up and what components are important to it.

7. *Key Partners:* In most cases, you will not be creating or developing your product alone. Most of you are supported by partners in one way or another today. Which partners are these? What do you deliver? Which partners are the most strategically important? Describe the ecosystem that you have built or want to build around your product.

8. *Revenue Streams:* After your product has been sufficiently described, you must describe in this field how you want to make money with it. What are your sources of income? License sales? Online trade? Product sales? Rental fees? Describe the types of revenue you use to earn money and the channels through which the money comes to you.

9. *Cost Structure:* Finally, this field describes your internal and external costs. These include personnel costs, production costs, host and operating costs, marketing and distribution costs, and so on.

As you can see, the Business Model Canvas is an ideal construct to easily describe, present, and discuss any Business Model based on the canvas and remodel it.

In addition to the classic business models, more and more digital business ideas are gaining ground these days. Therefore, the most important digital business models are presented in the next chapter.

2.5.3.1 Digital Business Models

Digitization is the basis for many new business models. Data is often the basis for this. Data is even referred to as the new oil; that's how valuable it is. At the same time, a paradigm shift has been observed for a few years now: People no longer want to "own", they want to "use". For example, music and movies are streamed rather than bought in the form of CDs, DVDs, and Blu-rays. Fewer cars are being sold in big cities because it is easier and cheaper to spontaneously order a vehicle including the driver.

Behind all these examples are sophisticated digital business models that precisely serve the needs of customers. In the following, some important of these new business models are presented, as they are very relevant for Business Development.

- *Freemium:* Freemium is made up of the two words "free" and "premium". In this case, the basic solution of an offering is provided free of charge, and special add-ons are subject to a charge. The model is also described in Sect. 6.1. The customer is thus lured with a free offer, only to be persuaded (with the help of cleverly placed purchase incentives) to pay money for the service after all.
- *Leverage Customer Data*: In this business model, usage data of a platform, software, or machine is collected from the customer at runtime. This data is then analyzed, assessed, and made usable with the help of methods from the fields of Big Data, Data Mining, and Artificial Intelligence (AI). Leverage customer data summarizes all the offers that companies can make to their customers on the basis of information from the data obtained. For example, a provider of air-conditioning systems can offer energy-saving tips and automatically optimized system operation for a surcharge on the basis of analysis data obtained from installed devices worldwide.
- *Add-on:* This business model is often used in the area of software systems. There is usually a core product that is sold to the target customers. The product solves a corresponding problem of the customer. Further, special requirements of the customers are then collected and brought to the market in additional software packages, which the customers can optionally buy in order to integrate them into the core software. These extensions are then sold separately as add-ons, generating additional revenue alongside the main product.
- *Cross Selling:* Cross-selling involves selling the customer additional products or services after the sale has been successfully concluded. These products or services are directly linked to the benefits of the initial purchase or open up a further area of benefit for the customer. This often takes advantage of the fact that hardware or software systems from a single manufacturer are usually better integrated with one another than systems

from third-party suppliers. This creates a sales advantage that can be boosted by paying appropriate attention during product development.

- *Guaranteed Availability:* This business model is based on the fact that the customer is no longer sold a machine, a special system or device, but rather the usage. The customer is contractually promised guaranteed availability of the service. The higher the availability (for example, 99.9%), the more expensive the contract. In return, the provider is responsible for verifiably ensuring this availability. To this end, digital services are used to monitor the condition of the machines and, in the best case, to automatically call a technician before a defect occurs, who can rectify the problem before it has a negative impact on operations. This is also referred to as "predictive maintenance". A well-known example is the Rolls Royce company, which is very successful in the field of aircraft turbines. They no longer sell turbines, but rather the service "jet propulsion". To this end, they use complex technology to ensure that their turbines provide the contractually guaranteed service at all times. For example, necessary maintenance is only carried out when it is really needed and not every time the machine is on the ground and no maintenance is actually required. This saves Rolls Royce a great deal of money and enables it to offer the service at a lower price.
- *Lock-in:* In this model, specific offerings are designed in such a way that if a customer chooses this solution, switching to another provider is very complicated, expensive, or even impossible. This is often the case with purely cloud-based offerings, where customers store all their data only in the providers' data centers and there are often no open interfaces for third-party systems to transfer the data from one system to another. The goal of such providers is to serve customers entirely on their platform and make it unattractive for them to migrate to a competitor with many adjacent offerings or a combination of hardware and software systems.

The digital business models described up to this point can be cleverly linked together and sequenced in such a way that you can develop your business step by step into the digital world. The process can be divided into three phases, which are explained below using the example of a supplier of industrial washing machines. In Fig. 2.4[3], the process is shown [27, 41].

1. *Phase 1:* To begin with, the latest generation of washing machines are equipped with new sensor technology. Here, the sensors can log, for example, the power consumption, the number of rotations of the washing drum, detergent consumption, and the selected programs and send them via a network interface to a central server of the provider in the cloud. The networking of machines with Internet-based services is called the Internet of Things (IoT). In the next step, the data collected in this way is recorded over a longer period of time and then analyzed. As an incentive to make their data available, customers

---

[3] Graphic based on [41]. With the kind permission of Materna Information & Communications SE, Dortmund / Germany.

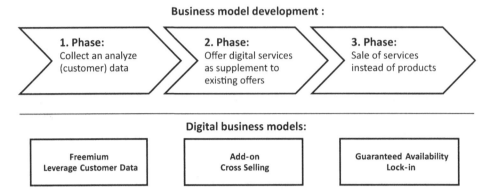

Fig. 2.4 The road to digital business models

can, for example, be offered a special app free of charge that visualizes the collected data accordingly and thus provides them with an overview of the machines used. This would be the freemium approach in combination with the Leverage Customer Data model. They use the data provided by the customer to deliver free added value in the form of the app. The next step is to then offer value-added services for a fee.

2. *Phase 2:* Once sufficient data has been collected and usable information has been extracted from the data using intelligent algorithms, additional offerings are generated from the insights gained. For example, a system for automatic detergent dosing and washing program selection can be developed, which can be retrofitted as an add-on in washing machines. The system generates further data that can be evaluated centrally, and the customer receives an evaluation locally in his app that also shows how much detergent and electricity has been saved. In the area of cross-selling, a subscription model for detergent and special service contracts based on the predictive maintenance model could then be offered in addition to the machines. This is possible because all relevant data from the machines is recorded and evaluated. In this way, possible defects can be detected at an early stage and treated on site.

3. *Phase 3:* In the final stage, the business model can then be fundamentally changed. To this end, washing machines are no longer sold, but the customer buys the "Clean Laundry" service. Here, the customer specifies his estimated monthly throughput of different laundry items and their average soiling. Based on this information and the data obtained from hundreds of machines worldwide, an individual offer can then be prepared, based on the Guaranteed Availability model, which guarantees the operation and wash throughput of the machines. At this point, the machines no longer need to be purchased. The expenses for maintaining the machines and possibly also for refilling detergent then lie with the supplier. The customer can focus on his core business and only has to worry about washing. In addition, the customer can now be offered a fully integrated web-based system for monitoring his washing machines, which in addition to monitoring

the machines also offers a planning module that optimally incorporates the surrounding operating processes of an industrial laundry. For example, the software could still offer an employee scheduling module and automatically assign employees to machines. In addition, further integrated offers are made that bind the customer ever closer to the provider and make switching to the competition more difficult and cumbersome with each step. At this point, the lock-in model kicks in and nothing stands in the way of a long collaboration (correspondingly good service is a prerequisite here, of course).

In addition to the business models described here, there are many others. Some important ones are explained below.

- **Affiliation:** This business model is a special variant of an partner model. If you sell products or services over the Internet, you can offer the so-called affiliate partnerships. Here, interested sellers can register independently and thereby conclude an affiliate contract with your company. This contract defines the partnership in detail. Mostly, it is about affiliate partners being allowed to offer your products and services on their own platforms or via social media. In the process, the actual sale always takes place via your web store. The affiliate partners can use appropriate advertising measures to ensure that additional customers, who would otherwise not have reached you, are directed to your store. The links that are used for this purpose on the affiliate partners' pages are specially personalized, so that it can be clearly determined which partner handed over the customer to you. For each successful sale through your platform, the affiliate partner is rewarded with a commission. The amount of the commission can be freely determined. Depending on the product or service, it ranges from three to five percent for low-priced, easy-to-sell offers and sometimes over 50% for complex products and services that require a lot of explanation and are usually high-priced. The affiliate model is a win-win situation for both sides: your partners earn a commission on successful sales referrals and have nothing to do with the actual products, services, or sales process, and you benefit from the sales reach of your partners.
- **Crowdsourcing:** With crowdsourcing, you move tasks out of your company and have partners do them over the Internet. Mostly such tasks are very small tasks which are often also titled as "Click-Work", because they combine a low level of difficulty with highly monotonous tasks and can be done with many monotonous mouse clicks. You can also outsource higher level tasks. This can go as far as outsourcing blog copywriting or design drafts for your products. There are now entire platforms through which you can incorporate crowdsourcing into your business. Keep in mind, however, that the quality delivered can fluctuate wildly and you never quite know who is working on your tasks at any given time. So be careful when using crowdsourcing, check the results regularly, and review your processes to only use this model when it really makes sense.
- **Long Tail:** In merchandise management, long tail refers to products that have been in your warehouses for a long time without being sold on a regular basis. They are also

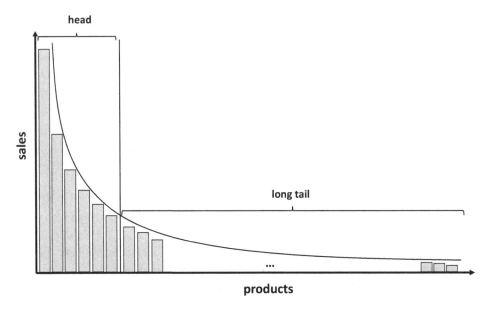

Fig. 2.5 Distribution of products sold by frequency

often referred to as slow-moving items. Nevertheless, companies keep such products in stock (albeit in small quantities) so that customers looking for these products can still find them in your web store and do not migrate to your competitors. The long tail business model is all about making precise recommendations for other interesting products by analyzing your customers and their buying behavior as closely as possible. With the products suggested in this way, products from the long tail are also offered in a targeted manner, thus boosting their sales figures. Figure 2.5 shows the model graphically. The business model is strongly data-driven, as a good recommendation algorithm must first acquire a lot of data about sales and individual preferences. Once this data is collected, the recommendations get better with each purchase. As a result, you increase your merchandise throughput, and the average shopping cart size increases, as many relevant products are displayed that the customer might not have searched for without the recommendation. For companies that operate successful long tail models, the Pareto principle then no longer applies, which states that 80% of sales are achieved with 20% of products. A well-known example of a very successful long tail business model is Amazon. You are probably familiar with the area under an item that says: "Customers who bought this item are also buying…". Here you can watch Amazon's recommendation algorithm at work.

- ***Open Source:*** Open Source comes from software development and refers to software that is programmed by a (loose) group of developers (sometimes also by companies) and made freely available. Thus, anyone can use it free of charge and view the source code. There are different license models that regulate the use of the software. They range from exclusive use to complete openness, which also allows further development of the software. The Open Source model is now also used in the area of hardware designs and allows the development of own products based on freely available component designs. Companies that publish their products (hardware or software) as open source release the source code, software, or hardware designs free of charge. Money is earned with adjacent offers. For example, software companies can make their systems available as Open Source, which can be used free of charge by private users. Business customers who want special service, regular updates, hosting (operation in a data center) of the application, and support can sign paid (maintenance) contracts.

- **Two-Sided-Market:** In this business model, a platform is made available on the Internet that allows third parties to transact their business. Here, the platform operator acts as a broker between two or more parties and cleverly brings supply and demand together via a digital platform. In doing so, the platforms are designed to be interesting and lucrative for all parties. The platform provider itself is usually not involved in the actual business and earns exclusively from brokered deals through advertising placed on the platform or by providing paid premium services. Well-known platforms that work according to this principle include Google and Facebook. They offer their services completely free of charge to end users, but earn money in the background by intelligently placing tailored advertising, which they can strongly individualize on the basis of the user data obtained. Other providers of such models include Uber, the world's largest cab company without its own cars, and Airbnb, the world's largest house and apartment rental portal without its own real estate.

- **White Lable:** This business model has been known in the field of physical goods production for many years. In the area of digital business models, the White Lable trend is currently gaining ground. In the White Lable approach, a company develops software that offers a specific customer benefit, but without the goal of selling this software itself. Rather, sales are focused on finding B2B customers who, in turn, want to use the software for their particular business. To this end, the software is customized for each customer. The software is not adapted arbitrarily, but only within the framework of previously defined parameters. This allows the design to be adapted to the customer's corporate design (for example, color scheme, logo, etc.). An example would be web-based software for companies that rent bicycles in big cities or in vacation areas. All these companies have the same or very similar requirements for an online platform to manage and run their business. Thus, a software company could specialize in developing a sophisticated platform for bike rental. This would be sold or licensed to local businesses. Customers can then use the platform in a customized way. It is not apparent to the end customer that there is a mass product behind the platform. However, this is also not of interest, as the customer can achieve his goal easily and effectively via the platform. In this way, all parties involved benefit from the white label solution: the software company can offer its software worldwide; local bike rental companies use an optimal, cost-effective, and yet customizable solution; and customers receive optimal service.

After you have developed your new (digital) business model and described it using the Business Model Canvas, you can move on to creating a business plan, which is extremely important for the management decision for or against a product launch.

2.5.4 Business Plan

The Business Plan is the central document that helps to describe the actual idea. Here, the focus is not on technical details, but on the overall economic context. The Business Plan can then be used to present the idea to management, where it serves as the basis for decision-making for possible implementation. A Business Plan does not have a fixed structure. However, at least the following points should be explained in detail (see [4]):

- *Idea:* At the beginning of the document, you should of course introduce your product or your service. What is new about it? What is the innovation? How do you differentiate yourself from the previous market? What problem do you solve? Provide the concrete properties and explain the structure and the implementation of the idea.
- *Target group:* In the next step, you should describe the clearly defined target group. What is your concrete target market? How is it defined? What distinguishes it? What sets it apart from neighboring markets? Is there a new market going on?
  The subject of market observation is discussed in detail in Chap. 5.
- *Market Analysis:* After that, you should present the results of your market analysis. How big is your target market? How is he segmented? What qualities do your target customers have? What needs do your customers have? How financially strong is the market? Are there any budgets for your solution? If so, who manages it? What is your competition? What are the pricing structures? The topic of market observation is dealt with in detail in Sect. 5.1.
- *Goals:* Next section will show what the goal of your idea is. How do you help the customer? What problem do you solve in which way? On the one hand, represent your goals qualitatively and on the other hand quantitatively. So do not just say what you want to do, but also how many customers you want to achieve in what time frame. Continue to provide relevant metrics that will help measure the success of your solution. This need not necessarily be all financial goals.
- *Resources:* Further you should outline what resources are needed to ultimately plan, build, and distribute the product. Which internal resources are needed in which departments? Which external resources are needed? What know-how is needed? The topic resources are presented in more detail in Chap. 4.
- *Costs:* Of course the costs have to be displayed afterward. Which personnel costs will accrue in the future? What are the costs for other resources? What are the costs that must be earmarked for marketing activities (for example, for advertising (online, offline, print), fairs, phone calls, roadshows, and so on)? What are the production costs? What

are the fixed and how high are the variable costs? Are there still hidden costs that are not obvious at first sight?

- **Revenue Plan:** After you have introduced the costs, you should present the revenue plan. What are your earnings? What is the price calculation? Is the product completely sold, licensed, rented, leased, or booked on-demand? Which types of sales do your product support? What does a short-term and a medium-term revenue plan look like? Are only direct or indirect sales achieved? When is a break-even point reached (when does the revenue cover the costs?)? All this is part of the market development strategy, which is presented in detail in Chap. 6.
- **Risk Assessment:** In this section, you should give a detailed look at all (identifiable) risks. Use well-known methods such as SWOT or STEP analysis. However, not only point out any risks, but also directly suggest ways of avoiding or mitigating these risks in advance. The topic of risk assessment is discussed in detail in Sect. 5.3.

Use the Business Plan for a holistic view of the idea. Be open to all advantages and disadvantages, all strengths and weaknesses, all opportunities and risks, and all costs and types of sales. Also, go into detail on how you want to market the product. In the best case scenario, present the complete product portfolio lifecycle: How will the new solution be integrated into your existing portfolio? How does it fit with your other products? What is the ramp-up phase? This is the phase until the actual product can be sold for the first time. How is the product treated and controlled during its active time? What is the end-of-life phase and how is it recognized? How is the product removed from the portfolio?

When creating the Business Plan, please keep in mind who you are creating the plan for. Is it only used internally to convince the management? Do you want to go to a bank to get a financing loan, or are you looking for investors who give you venture capital for your idea? You may also want to start a joint venture with one or more partner companies. This is a new company founded by several partners for a specific purpose, such as the development and distribution of a new common product. Take note of your target audience and consider when creating the Business Plan who needs which information at what level of detail and when.

After you have answered these questions and created your detailed Business Plan, it is time to introduce the plan to management. Here it can be decided early on whether further energy should be put into the project. If management decides to proceed with the project, it will be time to develop the first prototype.

2.5.5 Prototype

After a (first) Business Model and a (first) Business Plan have already been created for the new idea, you should start early to produce a prototype. Prototypes offer the possibility of having something "tangible" at a very early stage of development or of being able to be tested, criticized, and optimized (see [26]). This direct work helps everyone involved, since a pure idea has become an object of experience. Of course, this is much easier for a physical product than for a service or software. But also for the latter, there are possibilities of visualization. Thus, process flows of a service can be represented schematically, interactions of people and technology can be illustrated graphically, and software can be visualized, for example, with the help of so-called Paper-GUIs[4].

When working with prototypes, it is very helpful to take different perspectives in the assessment. The most important is certainly the customer perspective. For example, ask the following questions:

- How does the customer see the product?
- How does the customer interact with the product?
- Which (maybe not immediately apparent) application options does the product offer?
- What is the value impression?
- What advantage can the customer get from the product?
- What are the disadvantages or the risks?
- What else are the customers expecting?

Furthermore, you should take the perspective of the producing and executing unit. For example, ask the following questions:

- How can the product be produced in an optimal way?
- How can I achieve a high degree of prefabrication?
- How can the product or service be reproducible?
- What is needed?
- Who is needed?
- Do you need additional know-how, technology, or products?
- How does the product best come to the customer?

There are many more perspectives that you can take as follows:

- Management.
- Controlling.
- Warehouse.
- Purchaser.
- Sales.

---

[4] Paper-GUIs (Graphical User Interface) are drawn on paper program masks, websites, and controls. They make it possible to program without programming a line of code, to test program sequences and their graphical representations.

This list is certainly not exhaustive, but the idea behind it has become clear. First, test new ideas internally and put yourself in different roles. Later in the test phase (see Sect. 2.5.7), you will investigate what the real reactions look like and whether these correspond to your plans or whether you need to turn another round on the rack.

After you have created the first prototype and analyzed it, you can also do a scenario planning. Here, the new product or service is integrated into different scenarios that you will later find on the market. For example, go through various offer and sales scenarios. Which usage scenarios can you imagine? Do not just focus on positive scenarios. Play negative or even disastrous scenarios and record the effects. It may be possible to incorporate countermeasures in the product or in the enclosed contract to avoid major damage.

2.5.5.1 MVP

In recent years, a special type of prototype has become established, especially in the (digital) start-up scene: The Minimal Viable Product (MVP). An MVP is a very early preview of a future product, but one that already reveals its central features. Thus, hypotheses regarding customer benefit, customer acceptance, and operation can be tested at a very early stage of development. MVPs are often used as part of agile innovation processes and are not intended to represent the finished product in any form. MVPs are also often created at hackathons, which are intended to convey the basic solution idea at the end of the event and, due to time constraints, have no claim to completeness. Further, MVPs are not designed for mass testing. In the words of Steve Blank, "You're selling the vision and delivering the minimum feature set to visionaries not everyone". (cf. [5])

MVPs can be used to validate ideas at an early stage and find potential supporters (within the company or externally). Feedback from test users should be taken very seriously. If these early users do not understand something about the product and do not see any benefit or added value in it, the product should be fundamentally changed again. If the feedback is very negative, it is always an option not to pursue the product idea any further. This is naturally very difficult, since a lot of time and energy has already gone into the MVP up to this point. But if the future market fundamentally rejects the product, development must be stopped in time to avoid wasting even more resources. Since this is very difficult for everyone involved, this process is also colloquially called "kill your darlings".

In addition to the positive aspects of early feedback on a new product, there is also justified criticism of MVPs. The main criticism is that showing a MVP, and thus an unfinished and immature product, can cast a bad light on the company. This is a valid point and that is why careful attention must be paid to whom and in what setting the MVP is shown when planning the testing of an MVP. At no time should the impression be created that this is a classic product test with a market-ready product. Another point of criticism is that product ideas at such an early stage are often not yet legally protected. This means that ideas could be quickly picked up and further developed by competitors. In the case of digital products, a good idea can be taken over immediately in the form of a new app and made a little bit faster, better, or more complete in a central point, and users will already migrate to the competition. Such customer churn happens every day and it is often not the first app that later dominates the market, but the one that was a tad better at a neuralgic point early on and then rolls up the market from behind, builds up a large user base, and leaves all other providers behind. Thus, the timing of a test should be well chosen. In the best case, you still keep a few aces up your sleeve in early tests and do not immediately reveal all the details.

Now that you have used a prototype or MVP to make the product or service much more concrete and have tested it in various (albeit hypothetical) scenarios, it is time to move into the development phase.

2.5.6 Development Phase

During the Development Phase, the most promising idea is developed as a final product or service. It must of course be distinguished whether it is a completely new product, or whether an existing product is optimized. This can be done, for example, by adjusting or extending the actual product, but also by changing the target market or the entire Business Model. It should be clearly defined what exactly needs to be done. Thus, a concrete project plan is needed here (see Sect. 2.5.2). Decide who has which tasks to complete by when. Plan what resources you need to create the new product. Are more products needed? Special software, hardware, special know-how? Do you have all this in-house, or do you need to involve external service providers or partners? If so, who controls them? Also, make sure that the costs stay within the given budget.

Describe extensively the properties of the finished product in advance and determine clear measurement points and criteria from which you can later measure whether the product meets the requirements. Create early test plans and communicate the metrics so that all employees deliver the required quality in their respective areas. Also, assign clear responsibilities for the individual measurement results and record these in writing.

Then create a parts plan that clearly describes which parts the product consists of. For example, for a service, you can create schedules of responsibilities and communication and documentation flows.

In the areas of mechanical engineering, the car industry, software development, and many more, there has been a trend toward small and very small series for a long time. Some companies even build customized products. This is possible through clever variant management (see [1]). You define basic parts that can be assembled by the customer according to a modular principle and (almost) arbitrarily combined. The most well-known example is the autoconfigurators of the big automakers. They allow every customer to configure and order their individual car from a given set of basic and optional equipment. From the time of mass production without any variants comes the famous quote from Henry Ford: "Any customer can get his car painted in any color as long as the color he wants is black".

Professional variant management must be set up and maintained with great care; otherwise, there can be big problems in the production. Apart from the fact that through variant management money can be saved by a strict standardization of the partial products and their combination possibilities, you can respond thereby to individual customer requests and increase your customer satisfaction.

If, during this phase, you are developing a new product for a foreign or even an international market, you must meet many country-specific requirements and standards, especially for technical products. A good example is the power supply. There are many different standards regarding the voltage supply and the plugs. Furthermore, in many countries, special safety standards apply, the compliance of which must be certified by a standardization body before a product is introduced. For example, in the areas of food, medicine, toys, software, and machinery, there are some very strict specifications that you have to comply with in order to be able to sell your product in the respective countries. Plan appropriate adjustments for each market at this stage.

At the end of the development phase, the market cultivation strategy must also be determined. This is the core task of Business Development. It defines important topics such as the price structure, the marketing and sales concept, and the partner strategy. The topic is only briefly mentioned here, since it is presented in detail in Chap. 6.

2.5.7 Testing Phase

Once the Development Phase is complete, it is time to test the product extensively. As already described in Sect. 2.5.5 about the prototypes, you should test as fast as possible. This helps you to be flexible, to incorporate customer requests into the development, and to find potential weaknesses and errors at an early stage. Decide on clearly defined test points and criteria before the first tests. Normally, corresponding specifications from quality management should be specified. Of course, these templates must be adapted to your new product. Create very specific test plans with procedures, deadlines, and above all with fixed responsibilities. Only then can you ensure that the tests are carried out in the desired time and quality.

When testing, be sure to check that your product may be subject to any (industry) standards or other requirements, such as government or other jurisdiction. Take any test criteria very seriously and check their compliance. For some products, there must be approval at the state level. In the context of this approval often also the test protocols have to be submitted in a prescribed form. Inform yourself here early and in case of doubt get professional advice from an external consultant.

In this phase, pay attention to neat documentation of all test cases and their results. This is valuable data that will not only help you to improve the current product, but you can also learn from the mistakes and deficiencies for the next developments (see Sects. 2.5.10 and 2.5.11).

Try to get feedback as early as possible. First, present the product internally in your company. Invite people from different areas and allow any feedback. This gives you independent opinions that can help you to further improve the product. As the next step, you should talk directly to partners and customers. Perhaps you have very close partners, or long-standing customers, to whom you can show a new product at an early stage. So you will hear the opinion of your potential target customers and strategic partners who may later sell this product. The feedback from your customers is particularly valuable as they match the product with their specific needs. Here you will find out for the first time whether your market research has been right. Take the opinions of customers very seriously and incorporate improvements from (legitimate) criticism into your product. In the best case, you will even find a customer with whom you can develop your product together. This is a great opportunity for you because you can design a product exactly to the needs of your customer. But make sure that it is ultimately also a product that you can make available to other customers. Thus, the product must not be a tailor-made solution for one customer only.

After all tests have been completed successfully, in most cases you will branch back into the Development Phase. It then fixes found bugs and built-in extensions and made further adjustments. After that, it is tested again. You then go through this loop until you (your customers and your management) are satisfied with the product. If during the tests it turns out that your product has serious deficiencies that cannot be remedied, or only with excessive effort, the entire process can also be terminated at this point.

Once the product has been completed in the first version and tested successfully, it is time to test the product on the market before you go completely into the implementation phase. One of the tasks of Business Development is to find a customer together with the sales department who would like to use the product productively in its current state. You can offer the product to the customer for free or greatly reduced to find a real test customer. Maybe you will find such a customer among your good existing customers. Such a project is often referred to as the lighthouse project because you can use the hopefully positive outcome in the process. Talk to the customer at an early stage and ask him if you can create a reference report afterward. Here the customer can report on his first experiences with your new product and explain where the added value lies for him. You can then use this report very well later in the sales process because the so-called Reference Selling is often much easier. The reference helps the other customers to quickly understand the benefits and uses of the product. Thus, you can convince your target customers faster of your new product.

After this phase has finally been completed, the management must finally decide whether the product should really be put into "live operation". If this is the case, you can start with the Realization Phase.

2.5.8   Realization Phase

After the new product or service has been completed and all test phases including evaluation have been successfully ended, the actual implementation phase can begin. This phase, of course, is highly individualized again and differs from company to company. There is also a great deal of difference in the launch of a new product versus a new service. Basically, the following aspects should be considered:

- *Portfolio:* The new product or the new service is now ready for use. That is, the product can be included as a new and active item in the portfolio list. The current portfolio list should be accessible to all employees. This can be done, for example, via the intranet. In addition to a specific product description, it should also include price lists and other sales material, such as reference reports. This provides a quick and always up-to-date overview of the current portfolio. The management of the portfolio list may be a responsibility of the Business Development (see Chap. 3).
- *Marketing:* The new product must now be promoted in the target customer segment. For this purpose, the online and print advertising measures planned with Business Development can now be started. At the same time, for example, a press release may be issued to attract customer attention. Of course, the new product should also be listed on the homepage and described in detail.
- *Production:* If it is a physical product, production can begin at this stage. It is important to ensure that the previously defined quality criteria are constantly checked. Business Development no longer has any direct influence here.
- *Distribution:* Since the product is ready for the market and ready for sale, distribution can begin. This should be done first through the previously planned sales enablement activities. The sales department is trained accordingly by the Business Development. The advantages of the product are presented, the application possibilities explained, and arguments for sales discussions given. Furthermore, appropriate materials are issued. These can be, for example, finished product presentations or advertising brochures. All this helps sales to sell the new product optimally. Incidentally, this applies to direct as well as indirect sales.
- *Controlling:* As soon as the new product is on sale, the control mechanisms and metrics previously defined in Business Development must be used in controlling. This is the only way to ensure that key figures such as sales, turnover, and profit can be centrally recorded and used for management control purposes (see Sect. 4.6).
- *Companion:* If the new product or service is officially distributed, in many cases (at least at the beginning) after the transfer from the Business Development to the business an intensive support by Business Development is necessary. This is understandable as the product was developed here. In the case of accompaniment, sales may be intensively coached in the context of sales enablement. However, it may also be the case that colleagues from Business Development accompany sales in the context of pre-sales con-

sulting to customers and provide advice there. Furthermore, the presentation of the new product at trade fairs or lectures is possible. Business Development colleagues should be available as sales sparring partners during this phase and ensure a smooth start to sales.

- *Support:* If you want or need to continue to support your customers after they have purchased the new offering, you will need appropriate support structures. This can be telephone support on a hotline and/or service staff in the field. You may already have corresponding structures in your company. In this case, the relevant employees will need additional training, and possibly new employees will need to be hired. Define clear processes here and use a quality management tool to monitor compliance. If you have not yet had a support unit in your company, you will need to establish one at this point at the latest.

2.5.9 Communication and Internal Marketing

As new products and services are developed in Business Development and existing ones are developed further, the other employees are usually very interested in what is happening in the department. Especially if you have just introduced such a department, team, or role in your company, there is an increased need for information.

In order to keep all employees up to date, you should set up a communications strategy together with your internal marketing and communication unit, which initially reports on the staffing of the team and its tasks. Furthermore, a permanent communication process should be established, which informs all employees about what the unit is doing, what results it has achieved, and which goals it supports as part of the corporate strategy.

Communicate also the (possible) effects and changes for your employees and your company, which result from the work of the Business Development. Business Development should not happen in a quiet room. Otherwise, the impression of an ivory tower soon arises. Stick to the motto: "Do good and talk about it".

Richard K. Streich described in his change model the different phases of the emotional reactions of those affected (often referred to as stakeholders) during a change process. He divides each project into seven phases, which affected everyone as follows:

1. *Shock:* In the first phase, an absolute lack of understanding is brought to the change. Often the first rumors are already circulating and the coffee kitchens are already seething. "Surely that cannot be true ..." is an oft-heard saying.
2. *Negation:* In the next phase, the change is denied. It is tried to deny it.
3. *Vale of Tears:* After no one can deny the change, the big whining begins. Everybody gets upset and scolds about the change and the impact and claims that everything was better anyway.
4. *Acceptance:* Once the wailing phase is over, sufferers begin slowly but surely to accept the change. There is certainly no positive mood, but no one can deny the change.

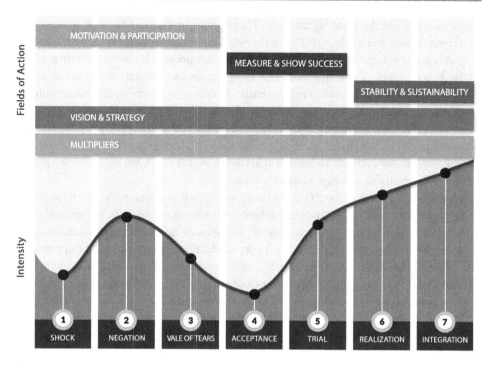

Fig. 2.6 The change model according to Streich with the communication fields of Materna TMT GmbH. (Illustration shown with kind permission of Materna TMT GmbH, 2022)

5. *Trail:* If the change is accepted and inevitably, stakeholders begin to deal with the new situation and try to find their way in the new situation.
6. *Realization:* In the next phase, those affected realize that the change has its good side and that the new situation brings with it a positive outcome.
7. *Integration:* Finally, the integration of change into everyday life follows. The stakeholders have arrived, feel comfortable in the new situation, and have incorporated the change into their lives as a matter of course.

Streich describes in his model, the emotional reactions during a change, which are inevitably going through each affected person. Only the intensity of the reaction can be influenced. In order to guide those affected as successfully as possible through a process of change, it is necessary to accompany the process communicatively with appropriate measures. To this end, Materna TMT GmbH has defined corresponding fields of action that have been coordinated with the seven phases of Streich's change model (see Fig. 2.6):

1. *Vision & Strategy:* This action field accompanies the entire change and shows the vision and the reasons for the change from the beginning. The vision is then used to derive

the strategy and the resulting changes. This vision and the goal must be continuously communicated and explained. This is the only way for those affected to understand the real reasons behind a change measure and go into uncertainty with a positive mood. To do this, create a one-stop shop (for example, on the intranet) that you can use to inform all those affected on a regular basis. Always provide the stakeholders with up-to-date information from the project. Continue to hold regular meetings and feedback sessions, and take the respondents' reactions seriously. Use the opportunity for personal communication and direct addressing via video as often as possible. As a result, all stakeholders are optimally informed at all times, which raises the mood for the project and significantly increases the chances of success.

2. *Motivation & Participation:* This field of action extends above all to the first three phases of the change model. Take the stakeholders with you, motivate them to constantly deal with the change, and anticipate the change. It convinces those affected of the meaningfulness and you show that you actively support the change. Give employees the opportunity to get involved in the project at an early stage, to exchange ideas, and to contribute their own ideas. This gives those affected the opportunity to influence the project (in part). This provides a strong identification with the change and ensures a positive attitude, since those affected are not the "helpless victims" of the change, but can actively participate in the project.

3. *Multipliers:* Find advocates for your change early on. You are looking specifically for people from the most diverse areas, who are positive about the project from the beginning and understand the benefits. Engage them actively in the project and in the communication and provide them with all the important information. These so-called change agents help you to communicate the change and they reach their employees again on a completely different and trusting level. The change agents should ensure optimal dissemination of information throughout the project.

4. *Measure & show Success:* Especially in the phases of "acceptance" and "trail", you should communicate the first (partial) results, the reached milestones, and quick wins of the change extensively and emphasize the positive effects. Let employees act as testimonials, giving credibility to statements and inspiring others. You can also organize special events and celebrate the results so far. It continues to lift the mood, rewards the past worries and efforts, and provides energy for the next steps.

5. *Stability & Sustainability:* Especially in the last two phases, the change needs stability. Old habits must now finally be overcome and new routines and processes must be integrated into everyday life. To do this, underline the achievements repeatedly and combine them with the vision presented at the beginning of the change. Explain the benefits and new possibilities. So you take the affected people successfully into the future.

By using a communication strategy that is individually adapted to the change, the failure of a project can be prevented and the actual goal of a project can be successfully achieved. Especially in the IT sector, the success of the project is often measured by the fact that in the end a new software has been successfully implemented or installed. Whether the employees understood the reason for it, or used the new software also profitably, is often not considered. For this reason, many IT projects fail: they are often planned and executed without the actual user in mind. Of course, similar things can be observed in many areas.

In the different phases of communication, you should use many different digital and analog media to spread the information. From a central intranet site, through blogs, video messages, infographics, employee newspapers, and small and large events, you can access all the stops of modern communication.

The task of a Business Development Manager, who should achieve permanent change, is therefore to motivate those concerned, to inform them, and to plan and implement suitable communication measures together with the internal communication unit. This ensures that the desired changes are understood and supported by everyone.

For example, together with internal marketing, design a monthly newsletter that reports on Business Development news. Another option is to set up a blog reporting news. If you want to communicate with all employees, you can also set up a special wiki on the topic that everyone can join. Furthermore, you can (if available) also use your internal social media network to distribute the information to your employees. Bear in mind, however, that this information exchange should take place permanently. Maybe even a quarterly dispatch of information is enough. But take the feedback, concerns, and ideas of your employees seriously and respond promptly to inquiries and comments. Otherwise, the communication is quickly one-sided and no longer taken seriously.

2.5.10 Documentation

Just as internal communication should accompany the Business Development process permanently, the process flow and its individual steps and decisions must be documented and stored centrally. Although this is obviously self-evident, the importance of documentation must be reiterated here. If important decisions are not documented in the right form, this can later lead to problems or misunderstandings. Furthermore, a centrally maintained documentation helps with future projects, since ideas, processes, business plans, contracts, or entire process steps can be recycled in the next iteration. This can save a lot of time and effort. The way in which you file the documentation is up to you and the rules and circumstances of your company. Maybe you use a wiki, maybe a central file server, or a collaboration platform. The important thing is that all key stakeholders have access to this platform and work together on the documents. Bear in mind, however, that good documentation must be constantly updated. This, of course, creates expenses. But they are worthwhile if the additional work that would be created by the permanent reinvention of the wheel is calculated.

2.5.11 Lessons Learned

As with any good project, you should also carry out a Lessons Learned session at the end
of the Business Development project. All project stakeholders should be involved in a table
course and should summarize the experiences of the project. In the meeting, all the actions
that went well should be mentioned, but of course everything that did not go so well should
also be mentioned. It is important to identify the reasons and to learn the result for the next
project. Hopefully, good actions can be built into the process and bad actions can hopefully
be avoided in the future.

Not only analyze what was good or bad in terms of content, but also find out at a meta-level
how the actual process has gone and try to learn from it.

For example, ask the following questions:

- What was the internal process flow?
- Have all steps been completed correctly, or have there been (justified) deviations?
- What was the (internal / external) communication?
- What was the internal cooperation (also team or interdepartmental)?
- How accurate were the market observations?
- How accurate was the Business Plan?
- What was the customer feedback?

If you have internal quality management, you should incorporate the results into your system.
So they are available to all employees. This allows you to increase the process quality of
your entire company step by step.

As trivial as it may sound now: Please document all results in writing. This is the only
way to ensure that the results will last and, hopefully, continue to be used.

After summarizing the important points in Lessons Learned, you can now use them
to customize the process. You should do this permanently, but always make sure that the
lightweight nature of the process is not lost.

2.5.12 Continuous Improvement

After summarizing the positive and negative results of the project in Lessons Learned, you
should use the results in the next step to optimize the actual process. Integrate the experience
and adapt the process to your company. Optimize not only the individual steps of the process,
or communication processes, but adjust the actual process flow on a meta-level. This may
result in different speeds in your business.

The improvement of the process is carried out after each pass. That is why this phase
is also called Continuous Improvement Process (CIP). This will increase the quality every

Fig. 2.7 The Deming cycle /
PDCA cycle

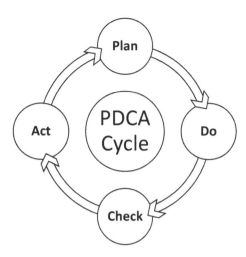

time. Think about what should be added and what might be left out. Maybe parts of the tasks can be outsourced to other departments or bought on the market.

The process of constant reflection and adaptation is also called Deming Cycle or PDCA Cycle (Plan, Do, Check, Act) (see [28]). A process is planned once and initially. Afterward it will be carried out and finally evaluated. The results of the evaluation are then incorporated into the optimization before the process is started next time. In Fig. 2.7, the cycle is graphically displayed.

But do not just adjust the process with suggestions from Lessons Learned, but also incorporate current market requirements and your company strategy. This ensures that Business Development always thinks in the right direction. However, with all the changes, make sure that the actual process remains lightweight and manageable. Otherwise, you will unnecessarily speed out the process.

2.6   Agile Business Development Process

In situations in which the target market changes particularly quickly, it can make sense to greatly streamline the Business Development Process presented so far and make it very agile. This may be the case, for example, during a current crisis or after the introduction of a disruptive technology. In this way, it is possible to react very quickly to the new market conditions and customer requirements.

The Agile Business Development Process is reduced to the essential components and focuses on the timely development of a new offering that has a high market relevance. The process is described below and shown graphically in Fig. 2.8.

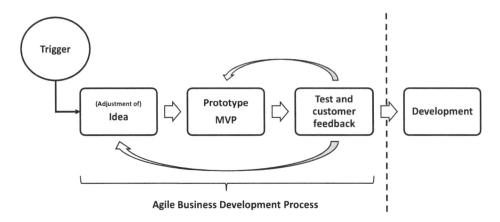

Fig. 2.8 The Agile Business Development Process

1. ***Trigger:*** The Agile Business Development process can be triggered by different events: Customer needs or entire market situations can change, a crisis can radically alter familiar market conditions, or a disruptive technology enables completely new business models overnight. All this means that the requirements of your target market and your customers change. You should react to this in a timely manner.

2. ***(Adapting the) Idea:*** In this step, an idea for a suitable product or service should be developed after an initial analysis of the trigger and its effects (for example, with the help of market observation, see Sect. 5.1). The creativity techniques presented in Sect. 2.5.1 can be used for this purpose.

3. ***Prototype/MVP:*** In the next step, a prototype or an MVP should be developed promptly in order to be able to demonstrate the benefits of the solution at an early stage (see Sects. 2.5.5 and 2.5.5.1).

4. ***Test and customer feedback:*** The prototype should first be validated internally with various people from different departments. Feedback from future target customers should then be obtained in a timely manner. In this way, it is possible to find out very early in the process whether a solution is being developed that will really find buyers later on. With the help of the feedback, it can be decided whether features of the prototype still need to be adjusted or whether the idea needs to be fundamentally refined. Initially, several runs are required here before the next process step is taken.

5. ***Development:*** After sufficient positive feedback has been received and the prototype has been optimized to the point where the test customers are satisfied, the actual development process begins. Here, the standard processes should take hold and the new product or service should be brought to market.

The process described here is intentionally designed to be very compact and flexible so that results are visible in a timely manner. You should adapt this process to your specific requirements and design it to deliver optimal results for you. This is exactly what agility is all about.

You can also design the subsequent monitoring of products and services in an agile manner and define corresponding triggers that initiate a review and, if necessary, an adjustment of existing portfolio items by Business Development.

In order to be able to discuss current and future innovation projects internally, the "Three Horizons Model" and the "Innovation Map" have proved to be useful tools. They are presented next.

2.7 Three Horizons Model

The "Three Horizons Model" was developed by the consulting firm McKinsey and first described by Patrick Brunet in 1999 as part of a framework on growth strategy (see [8]). It is based on the recognition that a company needs different types of innovation projects to continue to grow. In their projects, they found that innovation projects are not "equivalent", but that they have different goals, impacts, and target time frames. They summarized this finding in the model.

The "Three Horizons Model" makes it possible to talk about all of a company's innovation projects in a simple model and to identify their respective effects on the business. For this purpose, according to McKinsey, the projects are all in a state of tension between "run the business" and "change the business", i.e., the smooth operation of the current business and the adaptation of the entire business to new requirements (see Sect. 1.6).

In the model, all innovation projects of a company are assigned to one of the three horizons. The horizons are thereby mapped on a coordinate system. The axes have the following meanings:

- *X-axis:* This axis shows the time required until the respective innovation projects are completed.
- *Y-axis:* The value of the financial impact of each innovation project on the company is plotted on this axis.

Figure 2.9 shows the model graphically. The three horizons can be described as follows:

1. *Horizon 1:* Here, we speak of "optimizing in the core". This horizon includes all projects that will be completed from the current time until three years at the latest. They serve to strengthen and maintain the core business. The aim is to use innovative approaches to increase efficiency and expand the existing business.
2. *Horizon 2:* Here, we speak of "growing at the core". This horizon refers to projects that will be completed in two to five years. Projects in which new business extensions are investigated and built up are grouped here. Here, further offerings are enriched along the

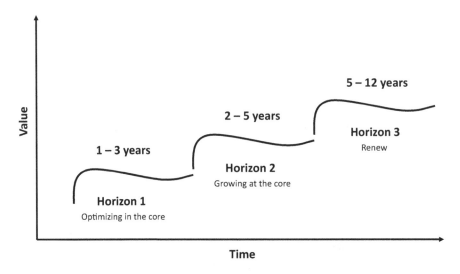

Fig. 2.9 The "Three Horizons Model" by McKinsey

existing value chain, which can be logically integrated into the business and comprehensibly complement the range of products and services.

3. ***Horizon 3:*** Here, we speak of "renewal". This horizon includes all projects that will be completed in five to twelve years. This includes all projects in which completely new possibilities are explored and completely new competencies have to be built up. This includes, for example, all projects that involve investments in start-ups or M&A activities (see Sect. 4.5). Here, completely new markets are addressed, entirely new business models are developed, and possibly decisions are made about replacements for business that is disappearing.

The time periods mentioned here are only rough guidelines that have resulted from McKinsey's analysis of many innovation projects. The time periods can be completely dynamic and differ from industry to industry. It can be seen, for example, that IT-related companies have much shorter horizons and are influenced much more often by leap innovations or disruptive technologies. The aim of the model is to summarize all relevant innovation projects of a company in one figure and to clarify their effective periods. There should always be enough projects active in all three horizons to ensure the continued existence of a company. The task of Business Development is to define, initiate, and actively support precisely these projects.

The "Three Horizons Model" only helps with the temporal analysis and the recording of the innovation projects. It does not allow an analysis of the content. The Innovation Landscape is recommended for this purpose. It is described in the following chapter.

2.8   Innovation Landscape

The Innovation Landscape is based on Gary Pisano's ideas from the book "Creative construction: The DNA of sustained innovation" (cf. [34]). It was developed by the company board of innovation and made available for free use under a creative commons license.

The innovation map is fundamentally divided into four quadrants, which enable a clear classification of existing and future innovation projects. The Innovation Landscape is shown in Fig. 2.10. The Y-axis shows the extent to which the new project is compatible with the existing business model. A distinction is made between the active use of the current model and the need for a new business model. The X-axis shows the extent to which the innovation projects are covered by the existing technical competencies. A distinction is made here between the utilization of existing technical competencies and the need to build up new competencies.

The individual innovation projects can then be entered into one of the four quadrants based on a subjective evaluation of the parameters of the two axes. The meaning of the quadrants is described as follows:

1. *Quadrant 1:* Incremental (re-)innovation—All innovation projects are classified here that use existing technical competencies on the one hand and the existing business model on the other. Thus, it is a further development of the existing business. An example of a project in this quadrant is the development of the next iPhone at Apple.

Fig. 2.10 The Innovation Landscape by the board of innovation

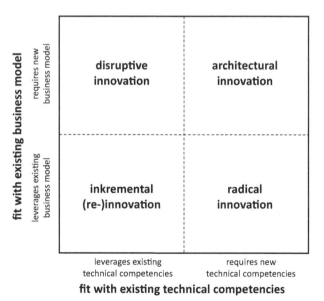

2. *Quadrant 2:* Radical innovation—All innovation projects that use the existing business model but require new technical competencies are sorted here. An example of a project in this quadrant is the development of e-bikes at a traditional bicycle manufacturer.
3. *Quadrant 3:* Disruptive innovation—All innovation projects that use existing technical competencies but require a new business model are sorted here. An example of a project in this quadrant is the development of mobility services at traditional car manufacturers.
4. *Quadrant 4:* Architectural Innovation—All innovation projects that require new technical skills and a new business model are sorted here. An example of a project in this quadrant is the development of blockchain-based services for a manufacturing company.

The Innovation Landscape helps to talk about and evaluate innovation projects with a common language. It becomes immediately apparent whether a given idea can be carried out with the current business structure or whether new partners, markets, or channels are needed (Y-axis). Furthermore, it can be seen whether the new idea can be implemented with the current technical capabilities or whether new (external) know-how, processes, activities, or resources are needed (x-axis). With the help of the Three Horizons Model and the Innovation Landscape, current and future innovation projects can be clearly classified and evaluated. Thus, these two tools should be used by Business Development as standard. In this way, the active and the planned projects can be explained (for example, in a management meeting) and their potential prerequisites, effects, and implementation periods can be presented.

2.9   Business Development KPIs

It is important to measure and make visible the individual Business Development activities and their results. Only in this way can the success and effectiveness of the individual measures be recorded, analyzed, and optimized. Business expert Peter Drucker said, "If you can't measure it, you can't improve it".

Key Performance Indicators (KPIs) are one way of measuring the results of Business Development. KPIs can, for example, show the results and capacity utilization of production facilities, sales, individual projects, entire business units, or a complete company. They are used by controlling and management as a means of monitoring and control. Well-known KPIs are, for example, sales, profit, and costs. Many KPIs represent the sum of many individual "sub-KPIs" at the top level, which are summarized for a management report, for example. For example, the KPI "Sales" can summarize sales in the areas of products, services, and licenses.

In Business Development, too, KPIs can be defined whose measurement allows conclusions to be drawn about the success of individual measures or of Business Development as a whole. To do this, the content of the relevant KPIs must be defined. Secondly, the period to which each KPI relates must be defined. For example, there are values whose analyses are sufficient on an annual basis and there are values that should be measured and evaluated per quarter, month, or even week.

Since the tasks of Business Development are located at the interfaces of innovation/research and development, sales, marketing, and management, many KPIs from these areas can be used. It may be possible to define new KPIs that apply specifically to Business Development by combining KPIs from individual areas.

The most important KPIs for Business Development are presented as follows:

Sales

- Number of new orders (for existing and new products).
- Volume of orders.
- Assignment to portfolio field or item.
- Number of existing customers.
- Cross- and Upselling Volume.
- Number of new customers.
- Cost per lead/new customer.
- Number of offers.
- Average supply volume (in the different areas).
- Number of (new) customer contacts (telephone, trade fairs, other events, online, mails, and postal).
- Sales Pipeline (customer, project, date, volume, and probability of winning).
- Win rate (percentage of offers won).
- Turnover.
- Profit.
- Complaints.

Marketing

- Total number of campaigns for new products or services.
- Number of social media messages (incl. likes, shares, views, etc.).
- Number of presentations (at trade fairs, (online) events).
- Number of mail campaigns (incl. open rate, conversion rate, etc.).

Market Observation

- Number of interviews conducted.
- Number of customer feedbacks.
- Number and evaluation of competitors.
- Recommendation rate.
- Quantified and qualified customer feedback.

Partners

- Total number of partners.
- Number of new partners.
- Sales through partners.
- Evaluation of partner status.

Innovation

- ROI (Return on Invest).
- Period until "break-even".
- Number of active innovation projects.
- Number of aborted innovation projects.
- Time to Market.

Mergers & Acquisitions

- Number of target companies under investigation.
- Number of completed purchases.
- Number of rejected companies.
- Average deal size.

Portfolio

- Number of (active) portfolio items.
- Number of portfolio items per BCG quadrant (see Sect. 3.1).
- Number of new portfolio items.
- Number of portfolio items removed.

Resources

- Utilization (personnel and machines).
- Costs (purchasing, storage, logistics, etc.).

Production

- Quantities.
- Unit cost.
- Material cost.
- Production time.
- Rejects.

Finance

- Budget (innovation, marketing, personnel, etc.).

Of course, there are many other KPIs that can be used to manage Business Development. Since the setup, processes, and goals of Business Development are individually designed in each company, not all of the figures presented here need to be used, and other additional or more specific values can be added. The important thing is that a clear picture of the performance and results of Business Development in a company can be developed on the basis of the selected KPIs and their observation periods. In doing so, make sure to capture and evaluate only the relevant KPIs. Not everything that can be measured is relevant. By clearly focusing on business-relevant KPIs, you reduce the effort required to collect them and make subsequent evaluation easier, since the results are not artificially complicated by superfluous values.

Together with Controlling, you can develop a Business Development Dashboard on which all relevant KPIs are prepared so that they can be checked at a glance. For example, a traffic light system can be defined for specific KPIs. For example, you can use a spreadsheet program or a special HTML page on your intranet. Here, the most important KPIs can be presented in a graphically appealing way in the form of charts, tables, and graphs. Such a dashboard facilitates control and enables a standardized exchange of relevant data. It may even be possible to collect and process the required data (semi-)automatically. Thus, you can access current data in your dashboard at any time.

Suitable KPIs should be selected for different Business Development tasks. Other KPIs are of interest for innovation projects than for monitoring and optimizing the existing portfolio. In the best case, the most important KPIs for the relevant areas are defined once and approved by management. In addition, a process should be defined together with Controlling that starts automatically as soon as a corresponding action is started in Business Development and activates the monitoring and reporting of the respective KPIs.

Business Development projects should be backed up right at the start with meaningful KPIs that enable accurate measurement of individual targets. In this way, an impression of the success of the project can be gained at any time and the short-term preparation of interim and final reports is also greatly simplified.

The goals for Business Development should be agreed upon and approved together with management. Corresponding KPIs for monitoring the (partial) targets can then be individually derived, set up, and evaluated. In this way, individual projects or the Business Development process as a whole can be continuously optimized. By monitoring the central KPIs, a continuous improvement process can be set up that leads to optimization of the individual areas with each run.

In addition to the KPIs from Business Development, central KPIs of the company should be discussed regularly with management. This allows further activities for Business Development to be derived at an early stage. For example, the analysis of the company's sales and the projection into the near future can be used to determine whether adjustments to the existing portfolio and its marketing are necessary or whether the portfolio should be enriched with new elements from the innovation area.

KPIs can be used not only to monitor and control Business Development as a whole, but also to manage the performance of Business Development Managers. For example, variable salary components can be linked to the achievement of set KPI targets. In this case, the targets adopted jointly with management should be challenging but achievable.

Conclusion for Daily Business

- Business Development can be understood as a role (with a specific task) and as a team or department within your organization.
- Create an individual role profile with requirements for a Business Development Manager. Pay particular attention to the soft skills.
- Before introducing a Business Development, think carefully about how to integrate it into your business and what specific and measurable goals you want to achieve.
- Define clear responsibilities for Business Development.
- Define a concrete Business Development process that is lightweight and flexible and can be quickly adapted to changing circumstances.
- Reflect and optimize the process and all processes on a regular basis.
- Use the "Tree Horizons Model" and the "Innovation Landscape" to plan and analyze current and future innovation projects.
- Define fixed KPIs for your Business Development. This way you can track the success of your activities and readjust them if necessary.

Portfolio

3

Abstract

The topics portfolio and portfolio management are very important to any company, because through the portfolio, the company defines the products and services offered to clients and partners. The topic is very complex and extensive. portfolio management is also a central topic for Business Development, as new and further developments of products through Business Development have a direct impact on the individual portfolio elements. That is why the topic is presented in detail below. This includes the portfolio structure and how you can organize your products and services. Further, the portfolio life cycle is described, which describes how the individual elements change over time. Finally, active portfolio management is discussed.

3.1 Portfolio Structure

Successful companies often offer their customers not just a single product or a single service, but rather several or even a combination of products and services. In order to keep an overview and evaluate the success and the reliability of individual products and services, you should actively manage your product portfolio. The basis for portfolio management is an unambiguous portfolio structure. It helps you to sort your products into unique categories, to rate them, and to determine how you want to handle each of the portfolio elements and their respective expressions.

As a first step, you should try to roughly sort your individual portfolio elements according to clear criteria. For example, you can sort your products according to the following criteria:

- B2B products (Business to Business)
- B2G products (Business to Government)
- B2C products (Business to Consumer)

© Springer Fachmedien Wiesbaden GmbH, part of Springer Nature 2023
A. Kohne, *Business Development*,
https://doi.org/10.1007/978-3-658-38844-7_3

- Market segment
- Target market
- Target country
- Sales strength
- Earning power
- Number of customers
- Product
- Service

Depending on your company size, it may also be wise to allocate the portfolio items in a first step to the respective entity units if they are clearly separated from each other. In a second step, you should sort the individual elements in each top group according to further criteria. Hereby, the items are often sorted by sales or by quantity. Classically, the products can be divided into, for example, A, B, and C products, with A products being the highest selling and generating the highest sales. C products generating the lowest revenue. Keep in mind that while this classification may be an indicator of successful products in the first step, certain products have a raison d'être, despite their low sales, as they contribute to the company's image, for example, or are very profitable.

Also note that there may also be portfolio items that are interdependent or that build on each other. These should also be grouped accordingly if possible.

After you have structured your portfolio, you should evaluate each element based on predefined criteria. This gives you a complete overview of your portfolio and the benefits of each element. In order to evaluate individual portfolio elements as part of a portfolio analysis, the so-called BCG matrix of the Boston Consulting Group has prevailed (see [20]). Each portfolio item is evaluated using two criteria:

1. *Market share:* This criterion assesses the absolute market share of the product in a given total market. This number can either be estimated or collected through a market research study.
2. *Market growth:* This criterion is determined by means of market observation and expresses how the market develops around the product. Roughly, a distinction is made here between a growing and a shrinking market.

If the two values are collected for all products, they can be displayed in a matrix. Figure 3.1 shows a BCG matrix. This matrix is divided into four quadrants, which allow a classification of the individual portfolio elements:

1. *Dogs—Market Growth Low and Market Share Low:*
   The Dogs (often referred to as Poor Dogs) are those products that have very low growth, possibly shrink, and have a low market share. It is important to identify these products, which are the potential losers. Dogs should not, however, be hastily removed from the

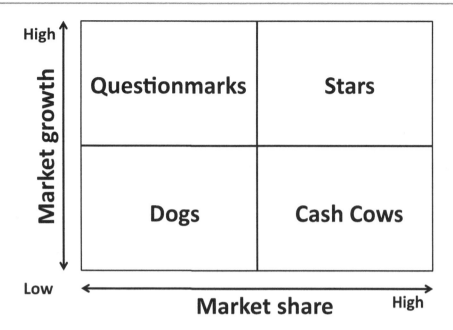

Fig. 3.1 The BCG matrix

portfolio, possibly bolstering the company's image. Dogs should be individually evaluated and permanently monitored.

2. *Question marks—Market growth high and market share low:*
   The question marks refer to products that are still low in market share but have high growth. They also have the potential to gain a larger market share in the short term. Therefore, these products should be specially monitored and steered.

3. *Cash Cows—Market growth low and market share high:*
   Cash Cows are the products that have gained a very high share of the market, but whose growth has stopped or has slowed sharply. These are mostly products that have long been on the market and have a loyal customer base. Of course, it is no longer possible to invest in these products. They run well and should bring the highest possible turnover with little effort.

4. *Stars—Market growth high and market share high:*
   The Stars are the products that have a high market share and continue to grow. These products should be all your attention. You should continue to invest in the development of these products and make them known through targeted marketing and distribution measures.

Often the valuation of the individual portfolio elements is extended by another dimension. The elements are not simply represented as dots in the matrix, but each portfolio element is weighted with the respective turnover. This can be illustrated by showing each portfolio item as a circle whose size is displayed in proportion to its sales. This makes it easy to see which elements are in which areas and how much sales they generate.

The BCG matrix was already postulated in 1970 by the founder of the Boston Consulting Group, Bruce Henderson. It is based on the observation and evaluation of the former market and economic system. More than 40 years later, the basic idea of the Matrix is still valid. However, according to BCG, there are some comments to note as the market has changed rapidly since 1970 ([37]).

Due to the speed of today's markets and the high rate of change, the individual portfolio elements move much faster through the matrix. That is why it is more important than ever to closely monitor the individual elements. This only works with a very fine controlling (see Sect. 4.6). Companies need to intervene much faster and evolve the elements from one quadrant to the next.

Previously, a large market share was equated with high profits. This has changed a lot. Nowadays, competitiveness and adaptability are much more important success factors. These factors should be included in the assessment of each portfolio item.

The goal of any business should be to have a balance between different portfolio elements in each quadrant. The high dynamics and fluctuation in the market demand a high number of question marks, which should be developed specifically for stars. This allows the market to be constantly tested with new products. If no success is in sight, the question marks quickly turn into dogs and should be sold or discontinued soon. In order to make the investment in the question marks, the stars must throw off a high revenue and capitalize the cows targeted.

Despite all this, Bruce Henderson's statement on the BCG matrix is still valid today: "Every company needs products in which to invest cash. Every company needs products that generate cash. And every product should eventually be a cash generator; otherwise it is worthless. Only a diversified company with a balanced portfolio can use its strengths to truly capitalize on its growth opportunities" (see [37]).

The right evaluation of the individual portfolio elements is therefore more important than ever. The sorting of the various elements into the matrix is the basis for an active Portfolio Management in the next step (see Sect. 3.3). Portfolio Management is based on the portfolio life cycle. This will be presented in the next chapter.

3.2   Portfolio Lifecycle

The portfolio lifecycle describes the typical phases that a product goes through in its lifetime. Each Business Development Manager should be aware of this lifecycle, as Portfolio Management is often located in Business Development and the activities are dependent on the particular phasing in which a given product is just in within the lifecycle.

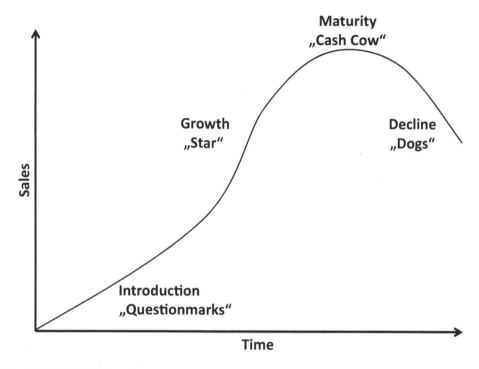

Fig. 3.2 The BCG Lifecycle

The model presented below, as well as the BCG matrix, was created by the Boston Consulting Group after years of study. It builds on the product classifications Dog, Question Mark, Cash Cow, and Star as described in the previous chapter and extends the consideration by an evaluation of the respective sales volume over time. The BCG lifecycle is graphically represented in Fig. 3.2.

This illustration describes how a product evolves over time in a given market. It should be noted that this model is certainly not applicable to all products in this form. Nevertheless, from this type of presentation, many interesting aspects can be derived for Portfolio Management. The model describes a total of four phases for an average product lifecycle. These phases are presented in more detail below:

1. *Introduction:* After the market launch, the product will remain in the introduction phase. The product remains within the BCG matrix in the question mark quadrant, as it has good growth opportunities but has only gained a small market share so far. In this context, you should focus on broad marketing activities to further promote the product and to progressively expand its market share.

2. *Growth:* Once your product has been successfully positioned in the market and has gained more market share, it is within the BCG matrix in the quadrant of the stars. The product

is successful and sells well. You should actively invest in further marketing in order to further promote the product. In addition, you should rely heavily on sales (possibly also through partners) to continue to actively gain market share.

3. *Maturity:* In the maturity phase, the product has reached its zenith in the lifecycle. It is very successful, sells well, but can gain no further market share. You should not invest in these products anymore. They run (usually) well and should be used with as little effort as possible to achieve the highest possible sales and earnings. Such products are classic cash cows.

4. *Expiration:* This phase is the last phase in the lifecycle of a product. The product is losing market share and sales volume is also dwindling. At this point, it is time for you, together with management, to decide to discontinue the product in the near-to-medium term and remove it from the market. These are classic (poor) dogs. Further Business Development activities are usually no longer useful here. In some cases, however, precisely such products can also be restored to their old strength through targeted innovation, or successfully positioned in a new market segment. This should always be kept in mind when you decide on the possible survival of a product on an individual basis before its final retirement.

As already indicated, the BCG lifecycle is a model. Not all products achieve the status of a star, for example. Thus, it may be necessary to initiate measures that will stop further investment in an unsuccessful product. You may also need to take the product out of the market early enough. Furthermore, the life cycle for services may be different than those for products or other merchandise.

In order to be able to determine exactly at which stage of the life cycle your products are, you need a very good controlling. Together with controlling, you should define fixed parameters, which are then prepared in monthly reports for you (and possibly also for the management). This will give you a good overview of your products at all times and, based on this information, you can take steps to optimize your portfolio.

Another way to show the life cycle of a product is the model of diffusion of innovation (see [40]). This model represents the buying behavior of customers over time. The model shows how a given product will find a larger customer base. The buyers are divided into five groups who decide to buy at different times. In Fig. 3.3, the model is displayed graphically. The following describes the different buyer groups:

1. *Innovators:* Innovators always want to be up to date. Above all, they are technically very well informed and like to invest in new products. They are educated and often have a high social status. They also face setbacks that can result from an innovation being floppy, flawed, or unable to prevail. The innovators make up about 2.5% of the buyer group.

2. *Early Adopters:* First time users are also very well informed and educated. However, they are a bit more selective in their choice of products and at the time of purchase than

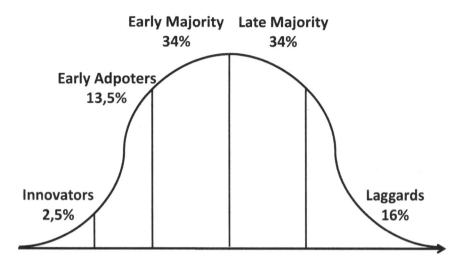

Fig. 3.3 Diffusion of Innovation

the innovators. First, you want to have proof (albeit a small one) that the product can be a success. They are well networked and talk a lot about new products. They decisively shape public opinion on a given product. The first-time users make up about 13.5% of the buyer group.

3. *Early Majority:* The early majority has above-average social status and often exchanges with the Early Adopters. But they buy a lot later than them. The early majority makes up about 34% of the buyers group.

4. *Late Majority:* The Late Majority accepts a new product very late. They wait until average comparison customers have already bought. They are usually very skeptical and do not have the financial freedom as the previous groups. They do not really shape the public opinion. The Late Majority also accounts for approximately 34% of the buyer group.

5. *Laggards:* The laggards decide last for a new product. They usually only do this when there is no alternative. They are often afraid of change and want everything to stay the same. They do not inform themselves about innovations and are usually financially low. The laggards make up about 15% of the buyer group.

For Business Development, it is very important to know exactly what phase a given product is currently in because different steps should be taken for each phase to move the product to the next phase as quickly as possible. Especially at the beginning, a lot of time and money should be invested in marketing and sales. Especially the first customers are often hard to find. Often it helps to talk to existing customers and to introduce them to the new product extensively. You may be able to get one or more existing customers to test the product at a discounted price and use it as a reference customer in marketing. Once the first phase, the innovator phase, has been overcome, you should focus heavily on marketing and sales (directly or through partners) to increase market penetration. From the fourth phase, the late majority phase, your product should be so well-known in its target market that you can shut down its marketing activities. Also, sales can be based on new products, since from now on, the customers will come to you, because your product has become a fixture in your target market. In the fifth and final phase, you also reach the last customers who have refused so far. Often they only do this because there is no alternative. At this stage at the latest, you should put your product into Cash Cow mode.

3.3   Portfolio Management

Portfolio Management is a very important task in companies with multiple products that are offered simultaneously to one or several target markets. All products and services offered to a market are considered as elements of an overall portfolio. This portfolio requires an individual structure (see Sect. 3.1). Within this structure, there are elements that are in different phases of the portfolio lifecycle (see Sect. 3.2). The task of Portfolio Management is to define what this structure looks like and to monitor which products are in which phase. The main task, however, is to accompany the individual products during a change from one phase to the next and optimally support the product, the market, and the internal departments.

Portfolio Management can be a separate department or a team. This again depends on the size of your company. Portfolio Management works very closely with Business Development and is often an integral part of Business Development for small and medium-sized companies. All in all, it is important to ensure that a company has enough successful portfolio elements at all times to generate the required turnover with the help of sales. For this purpose, the current portfolio elements must be permanently monitored and a potential expansion or adaptation of individual elements should be discussed with Business Development. Together with the product development team new elements can be designed that fit perfectly into the given portfolio. In addition, the results of the market observation from Business Development are used to see which requirements the market has and which elements from the current portfolio can be positioned so that they can cover the need. If gaps in the own portfolio are found in this analysis, they can be communicated and then, hopefully, successfully closed by new or changed products.

Another important task is to identify products that have reached the end of their lifecycle. This is done in close consultation with Controlling and Business Development. Once a product has reached this stage, many companies miss out on removing those products from their portfolios, often dragging on poor dogs that can negatively impact the results. In order to avoid this, portfolio items identified in this way must be discontinued after approval by management and then removed from the portfolio after a predefined period of time. Often this is not an easy decision as individual products have been very successful for years and have satisfied a large customer base. However, if this is no longer the case, or if an economic

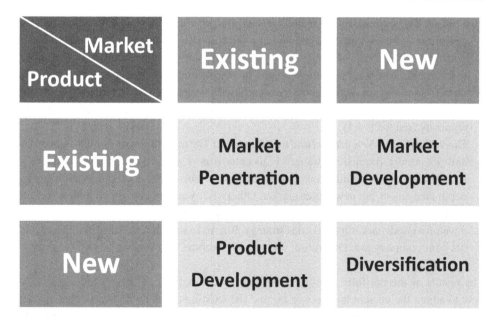

Fig. 3.4 The Ansoff Matrix

continuation of this element within the framework of the overall portfolio is no longer possible, this hard decision must be made deliberately.

If existing products are to be changed and, hopefully, improved with the help of Business Development, or if new elements are to be included in the portfolio, it will help to get an exact overview of the respective options. This can be done, for example, with the help of the Ansoff Matrix (see [44]). The matrix provides an overview of current and future products, helping to identify potential vacancies in the portfolio that are still unoccupied. These are the so-called white spots or white spaces. The structure of the Ansoff Matrix is shown graphically in Fig. 3.4. The matrix distinguishes between new and old markets and new and old products. There are the following four combinations:

1. *Market Penetration—Old Market and Old Products:* The right strategy for portfolio elements to which this description applies is to promote market penetration through targeted marketing and distribution activities, thereby gaining a higher market share.
2. *Market Expansion—New Market and Old Products:* In many cases, well-known products can be placed in new markets with little or sometimes even no hassle. These can be new segments in an already developed market, or even completely different markets, for example, in other countries. Here, it often makes sense to integrate experienced partners who are already successfully active in sales in the new target market. Again, targeted marketing and sales activities should accompany the new market entry.

3. *Product Differentiation—Old market and new products:* If you want to continue to operate in a well-known market, you can differentiate your product range by a clever portfolio expansion. This will allow you to use your prior knowledge of the known market and customers already acquired to place your new products. A new product launch should again be planned accordingly with the marketing and sales. As part of a market consolidation, you could also expand in this area by a targeted acquisition of the company (see Sect. 4.5).

4. *Diversification—New Market and new Products:* The most time-consuming, dangerous, and potentially promising strategy is to enter a new market with a new product. To successfully complete this step, you should have a thorough market observation and in-depth analysis of the new target market. Otherwise, you can quickly go under. As with the market expansion, you should look for experienced partners in the new market and develop a good marketing and sales strategy. But make sure that the story of your product fits your company too. Otherwise, you quickly become implausible.

The results of the portfolio analysis using the Ansoff matrix can provide information on how to adjust the current business or expand the existing portfolio with new elements. In doing so, and even during the initial sorting of the individual portfolio elements into the overall portfolio, you should always ask yourself how the respective product fits into your company portfolio. Is your portfolio consistent and comprehensible to clients? Or is there no recognizable common thread in the portfolio composition? On the whole, you should make sure that your portfolio is neatly documented on the one hand and on the other fits in with an overall story that your company wants to convey to customers. For each current and future product, always carry out an ecology check to find out how your customers in the various markets perceive your portfolio and your products, and what your customers and partners expect from your portfolio. Do not forget your competitors in the ecology check as you are usually not alone in a given market. Stay in a permanent exchange with the customers and their partners.

Changing existing products and their business models should always aim for one of the following three goals to differentiate themselves from other products on the market:

1. *The product should be cheaper:* This is the classic among the product customizations. If a product does not sell as desired, it is often on the priced down. It is important to pay close attention to how the market responds. Furthermore, you should pay attention to how long you lower the price. Maybe the reduction is also permanently planned. If your customers get used to a cheaper price, it is often very difficult to get a higher price without appreciably upgrading the product.

2. *The product should be more innovative:* Another option is to make the product more innovative. How this works in detail depends of course on the product and the target market. But use the results of market observation to change your product so that additional needs of customers can be satisfied.

3. ***The product should be specialized:*** The last option is a strict specialization. Hereby you search for a specific bottleneck after a detailed analysis of your customers and their needs and change your product so that it only serves exactly this bottleneck. While this will excludes a broad share of your target market, it will deliver maximum value to your target customers. This can be a very successful product strategy.

Another important task of Portfolio Management is to ensure that there is always a balanced mix in the different portfolio areas. At best, products should always be available in all quadrants. That this is not always possible in reality, of course, is clear. Especially new or smaller companies often do not have such a broad range of portfolio elements. But that is why you should study the existing elements and develop them further. At the same time, you should make sure that there is a good mix of sales types. Of course, this can vary from company to company, but do not rely on just one type of sales (for example, license sales), but always include other types of sales (e.g., accompanying services). In addition, Portfolio Management should constantly strive for a balance between the available resources (personnel, skills, goods, finances, etc.) and the products offered so as not to create an imbalance.

Overall, while adapting and changing your portfolio, you should always make sure that you always weigh a long breath when continuing a product and changing or discontinuing a product too quickly. Both can have fatal consequences. A recipe for success does not exist for the respective decision-making. Only a finely grained and permanent analysis of the numbers with the help of controlling and precise arrangements with the Business Development regarding the current and future market situation can serve as a guideline.

Conclusion for Daily Business

- Build a Portfolio Management system for permanent monitoring and customization of your offered products. This task could be located, for example, in Business Development.
- Develop a well-defined portfolio structure with uniquely measurable parameters for sorting and rating each item.
- Pay attention to the portfolio lifecycle and lead your products actively through the four stages to achieve an optimal balance between investment (product development, marketing, and sales) and sales or revenue.
- Ensure a balanced portfolio and revenue mix that is constantly matched against available resources.

Resources

4

Abstract

A central aspect of Business Development is resources. Resources include people, skills, know-how, partners, budget, and others. It is important to have a complete overview of the resources available and the resources to plan, to produce and to distribute new products. Thus, Business Development needs to know which resources are available for planned changes and where any additional resources that may be needed can be obtained. In the following, particular attention will be paid to the skills of the staff and the handling and planning of the available budget will be described. Furthermore, a distinction is made between internal and external resources, since both types are immensely important and should be included in Business Development. Another chapter deals with the field of inorganic company growth, as one possible way of obtaining additional resources is M & A (Mergers and Acquisitions). In doing so, new resources are made available to the company through the purchase of external companies or products. Finally, controlling is presented as an important resource for managing the business.

4.1 Skills

Business Development requires profound industry know-how. A Business Development manager needs to know exactly how their own business works and what skills they need in different departments to create and distribute the products they want. To ensure this, especially large companies have a so-called skill management. On the one hand, special roles are defined in the company, which assume exactly defined tasks, on the other hand, each role is assigned special skills with possible characteristics. Each employee thus fulfills a role assigned to him and his/her competence and experience are recorded in the respective skill group. As a result, employees can be quickly found with special profiles that are suitable for new tasks. At the same time, a so-called white space analysis can be performed with

© Springer Fachmedien Wiesbaden GmbH, part of Springer Nature 2023

A. Kohne, *Business Development*,

https://doi.org/10.1007/978-3-658-38844-7_4

skill management. It searches for gaps in existing skills based on requirement profiles. If, for example, a new employee in the production department is searched for a new project in the production area, a query can be made as to whether such an employee basically exists in the company, or whether a new employee with the required profile on the production line must be found externally. This employee search can then be initiated by the internal human resources department. In this case, the open position can then be advertised externally based on the profile you are looking for. You may also be able to use a Head Hunter to specifically find a new employee. If no new employee is hired, non-existent skills can also be built up through targeted training measures. Another way in which new skills can be integrated into a company is the M & A (see Sect. 4.5).

In the context of market observation, it is a central task of Business Development to constantly observe how the market is changing at this moment and in the future. These changes must then be assessed and the impact of these changes on the current business must be determined. It should also always be checked whether the right personnel with the right skills are available for the future requirements of the market. If this is not the case, appropriate employments and further training can be planned together with the human resources department. This is a very important task, especially in this day and age, as there is an acute shortage of skilled workers. This is especially true in the field of IT professions, which are becoming increasingly important as part of global digitization. So a good HR strategy is immensely important in the time of the "War for Talents", so that the company has the right resources and skills at all times (see [21]).

One point that has become increasingly important in recent years is the so-called soft skills (see [36]). These are interdisciplinary competences such as teamwork, conflict management, stress management, presentation skills, empathy, and problem awareness. Compared to the hard skills, which are acquired through education, study, and training, these are characteristics that are especially in the cooperation with other colleagues, communication with partners and before everything to customers come to fruition. Business Development Managers should have very good soft skills as their job is largely in communication with management, partners, and customers. But also the other employees should have good soft skills these days, because they are constantly in exchange in the increasingly connected world. This should be placed with great value in the selection of personnel.

4.2 Budget

A central topic in Business Development is the budget. In large companies, a specific budget per year is available for Business Development. This must be distributed to the corresponding projects by the respective team or deployment manager. If you want to have in-year special projects, it should be possible for the top management to hold a special budget. This, of course, applies only to really important projects that may have a big impact on the business.

The budget for Business Development can include multiple items. Here are some examples:

- **Innovation:** The bulk of the budget is certainly in the realm of innovation. Concretely, these are planned development projects, which were planned with a certain goal. The budget can then be used to pay for the internal employees who, for example, can no longer work actively for a customer or in production during the current project. Furthermore, investments in new technologies can be made from this pot.
- **Partner Management:** One very important task of Business Development is partner management (see Sect. 6.3). On the one hand, new strategic partners need to be found and integrated, and on the other, existing partnerships need to be maintained and monitored, since partnerships often have shared sales targets. Depending on the partnership, this can be a very time-consuming task. Sometimes it even pays to have dedicated partner managers for one or two partners. These partner managers look after the partner holistically. Of course, this creates costs that should be budgeted.
- **Marketing:** Partly, Business Development gets its own marketing budget, which can be used for targeted advertising, trade fairs, or roadshows. If this is not the case, Business Development should at least be involved in the planning of the central marketing budget so that joint actions can be planned.
- **Market observation:** Part of the budget should be invested in market observation. External experts can be engaged for this purpose, for example (see Sect. 5.1).
- **Travel:** A central task of Business Development is market observation. For this purpose, many customer visits should be scheduled. Because only here can the Business Development Managers know what their customers really want. In addition, many specialist conferences and trade fairs should be visited in order to keep an eye on the market and to be in constant communication with customers and partners.
- **Training:** As Business Development Managers must always be at the cutting edge of technology, a separate budget item should be scheduled for training. This may be, for example, subject-specific training, soft skill courses, or process training. Which training measures make sense is very individual and depends on the sector.

In companies that focus on new product development, there is usually a concrete budget for research and development in addition to the Business Development budget. Here, a distinction must be made precisely because the research department works independently and constantly develops new products. In this case, Business Development ensures that the right direction is developed so that market-relevant products are generated and successfully placed on the market with the right business models. Furthermore, Business Development builds and maintains an appropriate partner ecosystem, which ensures that its own products can be even better distributed or developed and produced with the help of partners.

Of course, Business Development generates costs. In large companies, which afford their own department or at least a team for this purpose, these costs must be transferred centrally.

Of course, this lowers sales or profit. Thus, the benefits of Business Development must be greater than the costs. In most cases, this is difficult to measure. In most cases, the developed measures only take effect after several periods. The costs incurred can, for example, be refinanced from the company profits. In the case of a large Business Development project, which may be strategically very important to the company, high costs may be incurred, which may also be financed by external credit or venture capital. Smaller companies often have to assign the task in addition to a line function. Thus, no additional costs are incurred on the paper at first. Due to the additional burden but the actual task cannot be met to 100%. This of course causes failures, which in turn can generate costs. This has to be considered very carefully when introducing Business Development in small companies.

4.3   Internal Resources

As already mentioned in Sect. 4.1, it is a central task of Business Development to understand exactly how the market develops and to align these requirements with the internal products and processes. All internal resources must be monitored. Only in this way can the limited resources be profitably integrated into forward-looking corporate planning. The task of Business Development is therefore to evaluate the existing resources for their meaningfulness and to look at the resources needed in the future and how they can be integrated into the company. It may also be the case, for example, that existing resources simply need to be recombined to achieve a new result. This requires the most accurate and up-to-date resource management, which allows a concrete overview of existing resources and their utilization or their presence. Basically, resources can be divided into several groups:

1. *Human Resources:* Human resources are the most important assets of a company. Among other things, they are responsible for production, administration, and sales. Of course, there are many other tasks, some of which are very specific to the company. Above all, Business Development should have a good overview of the personnel responsible for the production, planning, development, and distribution of products. For service companies, the focus is on the appropriate staff providing the services to the customers. In the best case there is a central Skill Management, so that each employee with its know-how and its abilities (for example, soft skills) is seized (see Sect. 4.1). This facilitates the overview of the current and future required personnel situation.
2. *Financial Resources:* Without financial resources, a business cannot work, and without budgets for development, a company will sooner or later be overtaken and deposed by market entrants. Thus, the budget of a company is a key issue for Business Development (see Sect. 4.2). While most of the company's budget will certainly be budgeted for personnel and/or production costs, every year an integral part of changing and evolving the existing business should be included. When planning this budget and designing these projects, Business Development should always be included.

3. ***Means of Production:*** Means of production denotes everything that is needed to create the final products. These include raw materials, consumables and supplies, supplied assemblies, partner products, machinery, vehicles, and much more. These resources are also very important as they are the foundation of the production process. In the context of Business Development, these means of production, their nature, possible further developments and alternatives should be considered permanently. Here also the purchasing and the production management should be involved.

In addition to the resources required now and in the future, there are of course resources that become superfluous due to changes to the business model or products as a result of Business Development. It must then be decided on a case-by-case basis how to handle the respective situation. If it is only a matter of means of production or raw materials, then this is certainly easier to clarify than if it concerns personnel. Here, together with the HR department, it must be checked whether the personnel can be equipped with the currently required know-how, for example through training courses.

In addition to monitoring whether all resources are available at this point in time, Business Development must also plan which resources will be needed in the future. Afterwards it can be decided whether these resources have to be built up internally (personnel), or reserved (financial resources and means of production), or if they can be integrated externally at a given time (see Sect. 4.4).

Often, especially in projects that need to be implemented quickly, new resources are needed that may not be able to build up fast enough internally. Furthermore, it may also be planned not to permanently maintain all resources internally. This may be due, for example, to the cost of storage. It may also be unwise to build up new employees for a specific area or project if they are just needed for a unique project. In addition, projects may sometimes or even always involve external staff, as they may be offered at lower cost than internal staff. In this case, external resources have to be integrated. This will be discussed in detail in the next chapter.

4.4 External Resources

As described in the last chapter, a company needs resources to fulfill its business obligations. These can be human resources, financial resources, or means of production (see Sect. 4.3). However, all of these resources do not have to be available at all times in the company, as this is often associated with high costs. In order to be able to plan and work financially, and to react dynamically to changing market requirements, companies often rely on external resources. In the following, some examples are given.

External resources are mostly used in the area of employees. Business Development should be aware of these opportunities and integrate them as needed. The following types can be distinguished by way of example:

- **Temporary Employment:** At temporary employment employees of a company are provided for payment to third-party companies. These employment relationships are only concluded on a temporary basis and the employees are never employed by the user company. This has many advantages for the user company. Temporary workers are often used, especially in manufacturing companies, to intercept seasonal load peaks, for example. Furthermore, temporary workers are usually cheaper than permanent staff. Sometimes agency work is also used as a temporary solution to quickly staff a new area. This is possible because temporary employment agencies often have access to a large pool of temporary workers, which can be used very quickly.

  Temporary workers must be trained. Thus, not to be underestimated expenses apply. In addition, there are sometimes problems, as some companies specifically use temporary workers to keep the total labor costs as low as possible. Often temporary workers are not well treated, and it is difficult for them to integrate into the lending company. This can quickly create a two-class society, which can have a negative effect on the work performance. However, temporary work can be a sensible means when used, for example, to cushion production fluctuations or special market requirements.

- **Freelancers:** Freelancers are not employed in the company, but they are self-employed. They are hired for special tasks and receive a fee for this. In this case, a temporary contract on a service basis, or an open-ended contract with an owed trade can be agreed.

  Freelancers are often specialists who have in-depth know-how in specific technologies, processes, or consultancy. Partly freelancers are also sold to customers. For example, freelancers can be used in an IT project in order to be able to offer a major project to the end customer from a single source. In this construct, the freelancers are subcontractors of the provider and bring special know-how into a project. The company that hired the freelancers acts as a general contractor towards the end customer (see [19]).

  Freelancers are often used to solve a specific task internally or externally at short notice. In some cases, freelancers are also hired after several assignments. For the company, this is cheaper in the long run and it gives the employee security.

- **Offshoring:** Offshoring relocates internal business or entire business units overseas. Mostly financial reasons are the motivation (see [23]). In the classical sense, the task or division remains part of the company and only the location is relocated. This is often done because of lower pay levels in other countries. Often, however, classic offshoring is combined with outsourcing (see below) to save further costs and to consume only one service instead of producing it yourself. Tasks that are often operated via offshoring include IT operations, IT support, customer support (for example, a hotline), personnel administration, and accounting. Another very common use of offshoring is production. Large manufacturing companies often operate their production in Asian countries to keep production costs as low as possible.

  Offshoring is often used in IT to run your own services or entire data centers. Often software developers are also used who live in countries with low labor costs. In some cases, end customers even set specifications for IT projects that stipulate that a certain amount of development must be handled via offshoring or nearshoring in order to reduce project costs.

Its i not as easy as it may sound at first. The quality delivered is the most important criterion. However, this can fluctuate greatly and must be permanently monitored. Of course, this will again generate costs that have to be counted against the savings made by offshoring. Another major problem lies in the sometimes large cultural differences between employees in different regions of the world. For example, employees in India must be managed and controlled differently than employees in Germany or America. This must be clear to the company, which wants to use offshore or nearshoring. In addition, the legal framework needs to be extensively scrutinized, as each country has different laws (for example, data protection law, occupational safety, etc.).

- *Nearshoring:* Nearshoring is very similar to offshoring (see [23]). It differs only in the choice of countries in which the tasks can potentially be relocated. For North America, for example, the South American countries come into question. From a German point of view, the eastern European countries come into question, since they have a significantly lower wage level than Germany.

  Nearshoring has the advantage over offshoring that geographic distances are not so big, which is often an advantage in day-to-day business, as important meetings can be conducted on-site at a lower cost. The biggest advantage, however, lies in the fact that the cultural differences are not as big as in offshoring and thus employee leadership is often more easy.

- *Outsourcing:* Outsourcing often assigns entire departments or tasks to an internal or external service provider. This contractually guarantees the provision of the services under measurable conditions. Outsourcing makes it possible to obtain a service without having to produce it yourself. This reduces the company's capital costs (CAPEX, Capital Expenditures) because, for example, it eliminates the need to purchase hardware and software. Furthermore, the personnel costs are reduced, since the service is no longer provided with own staff. However, operational expenses (OPEX, Operational Expenditures) increase by purchasing the service. Services or divisions that are often outsourced are, for example, IT operation, IT support, customer hotline, human resources management, and accounting. However, core processes should never be outsourced from the actual value creation, as this is the real added value of the company with which the turnover is generated in the market. So usually tasks are outsourced, which bring no real business value and keep the company from the actual core business.

- *External Sales:* Sometimes own sales are not enough to distribute the products or services in the desired quantity. In that case, external sales resources can be used at short notice. Freelancers can be employed here, or new distribution partners can be sought on the market (also internationally). Frequently, corresponding partner contracts are not concluded immediately, but it is first worked together for some time on a basis of trust, before a bilateral agreement is concluded. Thus, new distribution channels can be opened at short notice.

In addition, it is also possible to work with companies that specialize in telephone acquisition. These so-called call centers can support after a short training phase with the acquisition of new customer. Of course, this cannot be done in every area and in every industry, as it often requires deep industry or product know-how. However, it is often sufficient for call centers to only generate first-time appointments for their own sales staff, who then bring with them the necessary sales know-how. In this way, customer appointments can be generated quickly, especially for new products.

If external resources are used over a longer period of time or even strategically integrated into production, suppliers often become partners. These can then be tied to the company through special contracts. Also, special discount conditions are often coupled with large or long-term purchase quantities. Pay attention to a well-functioning partner management (see 6.3). Please keep in mind that it is extremely important to centrally monitor and control the external resources. This often involves using a resource management. Sometimes this is found in central purchasing, but sometimes also in bookkeeping. Business Development should keep in mind which external resources are being used to derive the areas in which own resources would be necessary and worthwhile. On the other hand, Business Development can ensure that much-needed resources that are not yet available in the company are externally integrated. Here, Business Development can assist in selecting and managing suitable resource suppliers or partners.

Another way to integrate external resources is through a joint venture. Here, two or more companies get together and start a new company for a common purpose. This can have many reasons. For example, one company may have great technical know-how, and the second company specializes in production or distribution. Together, a new company can be founded that combines both advantages without the companies having to build up or buy the missing know-how themselves.

In addition, it is also possible to integrate external resources into the company through a company purchase. This is summarized under the term M & A (Mergers and Acquisitions). The next chapter describes this situation in detail.

4.5   Mergers & Acquisitions

Mergers & Acquisitions summarizes two major areas of corporate development. On the one hand, the mergers, in which two or more companies merge into a single new company in order to work together on the market. Second, the acquisitions in which a company or part of a company is bought entirely by another company (see [7]). In the second case, we also talk about a carve out. These areas are also of interest for Business Development, since, for example, the portfolio can be expanded or the sales reach increased by a strategic acquisition of a company. Business Development can be used as an idea generator. Part of the responsibility for the entire M & A process lies in Business Development. This varies from company to company and also depends on company size and frequency of M & A activity.

There are various reasons to buy a company. The most important ones are the following three:

1. *Customers:* A company is taken over to increase the active customer base by leaps and bounds. Through the acquisition, synergies always arise in sales. Thus, both portfolios can now be offered to both customer portfolios. This increases the cross-selling potential. This means that additional products from the existing portfolio will be sold to an existing customer in addition to the previously purchased product.
2. *Technology:* A company is acquired because it has a particular technology that provides the buying company with a competitive advantage in the marketplace. For example, this technology may be in a particular production technique or in a software solution. Through the acquisition, the buying company can also profitably use this technology and thereby, for example, produce faster or enhance an existing product.
3. *Staff:* A company is taken over because it has good or specially trained personnel. As a result, specific know-how can quickly be transferred to the buying company. This may result in market or sales benefits.

All in all, the M & A area (above all the parts of business) can be divided into three phases, which are briefly presented in the following:

1. *Pre-Phase:* In the first phase, you should first consider why another company or technology should be purchased at all. Here, the decision should be given by the strategic management. At the same time, a target profile should be drawn up, which specifies exactly what kind of company or technology is being searched for, where it is located, and what the possible pricing framework looks like. After that, the unit that is responsible for this task (for example, Business Development) can start looking for potential candidates. This is also referred to as Target Screening. Once a target has been identified, a rough assessment can be performed. Here, the most important basic data of the company potentially to be purchased is determined and compared with the specifications from the management. If the target company is shortlisted, first concrete steps can be planned. In the following, it is assumed that the target company is even for sale. After initial discussions have been held with the target company and the interest has been expressed, the planning of the actual process can begin. Here, the planning of the M & A organization is carried out first. This means that internal responsible persons are designated for the areas of legal, finance, and content specialists who accompany the next process steps. Furthermore, a process owner must be defined. In the next step, preliminary contracts can be closed. The two most important are the NDA (Non Disclosure Agreement), which regulates the confidentiality of the respective parties and the LOI (letter of intent)) that states that there is a serious purchase intent.

2. ***Transaction Phase:*** The second phase starts with DD (due diligence). This is a deep analysis of the financial ratios of the company to buy. Following the DD, the detailed negotiations can be started. It is agreed on the actual purchase price. There are different possibilities. In the standard case, the entire purchase amount may become due on a due date. But there are also performance-related payouts that are paid out over years. In these so-called earn-out models, a payment is negotiated which, in relation to a defined business case, pays premiums that depend on the (joint) success of the companies. Of course, combinations or other purchase price models are possible. Once the purchase price has been defined, work can start on the actual purchase contract. In most cases, external management consultants and law firms are involved in order to ensure process security.
   Once the contract of sale (SPA, Share Purchase Agreement) is finalized, the management (the board, the shareholders, etc.) must also internally decide to proceed with the takeover. If all decisions are complete, the contract can be signed. After an antitrust investigation, the takeover can be legally concluded. This refers to the closing.
3. ***Integration Phase:*** In the third phase, the two companies will be integrated. This is referred to as PMI (Post Merger Integration). This is the longest and most complex phase as two previously independent companies need to be integrated. Human resources must be pooled, management must be reorganized, systems and technology must be harmonized, production must be integrated, internal and external communication must be adapted, commercial integration must be completed and much more. All in all, this is a complex change project where the most important thing is to take the employees of both companies and show them the benefits and opportunities of integration. In addition, synergies must be raised in this phase. These can arise through a merger of locations or through joint sales. But also the use of a uniform billing system or a joint production can bring significant cost advantages. This must be checked individually with every takeover and then implemented accordingly in order to really take full advantage of a takeover.

4.6   Controlling

Controlling is a central function in the operational procedure. Controlling creates business transparency in the company and supports the management in the forward-looking decision-making. In doing so, the department works with the data from the accounting department and helps to balance the achievement of corporate goals and strategic objectives as well as project goals (see [38]).

Controlling is an important internal point of contact for Business Development since all business-relevant figures come together here and are evaluated regularly. Together with the controlling department, Business Development can evaluate in which customer segments which countries which products are sold well and where this is not the case. Furthermore, internal trend analyzes can be created, which help to guide the internal portfolio through the life cycle (see Chap. 3). Thus, Business Development and controlling must work together closely to define metrics that allow for the control of ongoing projects and current products, while allowing for future analysis that allows conclusions from future portfolio adjustments to be made from the market analysis information. Care should always be taken to ensure that the costs and benefits of the analysis are meaningful.

When developing and launching a new product or service, Business Development should always include controlling. This ensures from the beginning that the profitability is measured and monitored. For this purpose, the two departments must coordinate accordingly and set the required monitoring measures early. Furthermore, defined reports should be created at regular intervals and evaluated together. This allows the portfolio to be optimally managed and adapted to market conditions.

Conclusion for Daily Business

- Make sure you always have a complete overview of all available resources with their respective workloads. Also determine what resources will be needed in the future and plan appropriate measures (training, recruitment, credit negotiations, etc.).
- Get active skill management. Your employees and their skills are the real capital of your company. Handle this capital with care and plan training and staff development to always have the right people with the right knowledge.
- Plan a special budget for Business Development. Pay attention to a holistic cost analysis.
- Cleverly use internal and external resources to optimize your cost structures and be agile on the market.
- Business acquisitions or mergers (M & A) help you grow fast. This inorganic growth can have three reasons: customers, technology, and/or staff.
- Business Development should work very closely with Controlling. This guarantees that all activities can be measured and managed right from the start using the right (financial) parameters.

Target Market

5

Abstract

An important task of Business Development is to have a good overview of the current market situation. This overview is very important as new or existing products must ideally be positioned in the target market, to achieve high sales. In order to find and understand this target market for the first time, a market analysis is necessary. Here, either through own online and offline research or by external market research companies, the market, its participants, the products represented in it, the customers with their requirements and the competitors are analyzed extensively. In the next step, the defined target market can then be divided into individual market segments. This is helpful because different market segments have different requirements and different target customers who may need a different sales approach. Afterwards, the defined target market can be examined with the help of a risk analysis, which shows on the one hand, which chances the market offers, on the other hand also shows, which risks arise. These should be thoroughly understood and best avoided. Another task of Business Development can also be the internationalization of a product. A new market in one or more new countries where a distribution is worthwhile is searched for a known market. Here, many details and regulations have to be taken into account in order to create a successful market entry.

5.1   Market Observation

Permanent market observation is an ongoing task for Business Development. Since the main task of Business Development is to constantly improve the company and the respective products and services and to adapt them to the constantly changing customer requirements, it must be clear at all times how the market in which the company finds itself is currently behaving and how it will develop in the future.

© Springer Fachmedien Wiesbaden GmbH, part of Springer Nature 2023   99
A. Kohne, *Business Development*,
https://doi.org/10.1007/978-3-658-38844-7_5

Market observation is a sub-discipline of market research. In contrast to market research, it relates to a period of time rather than a specific point in time. Market observation attempts to predict future market behavior on the basis of historical data, survey data and other technical and socio-economic factors. A distinction is made in market observation between primary and secondary observation. In primary observation, the data to be evaluated is collected by the company itself. This can be done, for example, with the help of surveys. In secondary observation, data from freely available sources (for example, studies and trend barometers) are evaluated and condensed accordingly. Business Development can carry out basic market observation. However, if in-depth analyses are to be carried out that will serve as the basis for a new corporate strategy, an external company should be commissioned to carry out comprehensive market observation. Such companies often access large databases with many values from a wide range of industries and have their own call centers that specialize in surveys.

Furthermore, a distinction is made between qualitative and quantitative market observation. Qualitative observation uses classic interviews and surveys with free-text fields. The results are summarized in the form of customer statements and feedback. Quantitative market observation records opinions, statements, and information in the form of figures. Results and assessments can be recorded using scales, traffic light systems, or rating stars.

Market observations can be carried out over different periods of time. Short-term evaluations help to get a quick overview of a given market. However, since a deeper understanding of the specific market is often lacking, the period of investigation may be too short or the wrong people may be interviewed. Also, the sample size may be chosen too small. In the worst case, this can lead to biased or incorrect results, which can lead to an incorrect assessment of the market situation. Long market observations provide much more reliable results, as an understanding of the market, its conditions and its specialties is built up over a long period of time. Unfortunately, there is often not enough time or money to conduct long-term studies. Thus, a good balance has to be found between cost and effort as well as meaningfulness of the observation.

In the case of a market observation, a fundamental distinction can be made between "questioning" and "observing":

- *Questioning:* Here, people from the selected market are actively surveyed. This can be done, for example, with the help of interviews, surveys, or special focus groups. The surveys can be conducted in person, by telephone, or via the Internet. The results can then be evaluated qualitatively and/or quantitatively.
- *Observing:* Here, people in the target group are observed while shopping or having conversations, for example. This can be recorded in a scenario using cameras and evaluated later. There are also special devices that record the eye movements of the subjects. This can be used, for example, to evaluate where they look in a shop window, on a shelf or in an advertisement in order to draw conclusions about interest that is not directly expressed and possible buying behavior.

In principle, market observation should provide information about the type of market in which the company operates or about the behavior of a market in which the company wants to make new inroads. Key trends should be identified that show what moves the market and, in particular, the customers. What market forces are active? What macroeconomic forces are at work? What specific industry forces are at work? What political influences are at work? What constraints or legal requirements are in place? What bottlenecks currently exist and what are seen for the future?

The aim of market research is to gain the best possible understanding of the relevant market and its participants. This includes an overview of the overall situation of the target market, customers' opinions of their own company and the products and services it offers, customers' buying behavior, satisfaction and loyalty, the available investment volume and willingness to invest, an overview of market competitors and their price structures, an evaluation of the impact of the company's own advertising and an assessment of its own market position.

Market observation is intended to identify opportunities for new products and services at an early stage, make trends visible and help identify risks at an early stage so that they can be avoided. Building on the market observation, adjustments can possibly be made to the offering and, if necessary, the marketing and sales strategy can be adapted to the changing situation.

Market monitoring should be aligned with the target market. However, this also means that the target market must be precisely defined beforehand. Only then can the parameters needed to assess the current and future situation of the market be collected and examined.

In doing so, also examine how purchasing power is developing in your target market, what cultural changes are playing a role and, of course, how your market competitors are positioning themselves and how they are adapting to the changing circumstances. One simple way to do this is to be in close exchange with your own customers and partners. Ask them how they see the market right now and what they would like to see in the future. Furthermore, you should read industry-standard trade media and visit trade fairs and conferences. This will give you a good overview of the target market.

You should also use your market observation to find out which technologies will play a major role in your target market in the future, so that you can deal with them at an early stage and consider whether these technologies can be profitably integrated into your business. Furthermore, you should scan the market for potential new partners. In this way, you can permanently update your ecosystem.

The process of a market observation is based on that of a classic empirical study and can be divided into eleven phases (cf. [18]):

1. *Defining the problem:* At the beginning, the underlying problem is precisely defined and the target market to be investigated is defined. This can prevent the results from becoming distorted or completely unusable.

2. *Defining the research design:* Defining the design involves determining what type of market observation is to be involved. For example, should people be interviewed openly on the street or should a special experiment be set up in a research laboratory.

3. *Defining the sources of information:.* This defines which sources are to be used. For example, first-hand surveys can be used as well as results from experiments that have already been conducted.

4. *Definition of the performer:* This step defines who will ultimately carry out the observation. Here it is determined whether the task is to be handled by the company's own personnel, whether a special market research company is to be called in or whether the company is to cooperate with a university.

5. *Determining the data collection method:* The next step is to define how the data will be collected. This can be done using surveys, interviews, or focus groups, for example.

6. *Sample selection:* Next, the type and size of the sample to be studied are determined. Care must be taken to ensure that the sample size is chosen so that the result is statistically relevant and allows a realistic assessment of the real situation. Samples that are too small or incorrectly selected can have a negative influence on the result.

7. *Design of the survey instrument:* This is where the actual survey is prepared. For example, the specific questions for an interview or survey are developed, evaluated, sorted, and tested.

8. *Carrying out the data collection:* In this step, the actual survey is performed.

9. *Editing and coding the data:* After all results have been recorded and secured, this step involves editing the results so that they can be analyzed. For example, oral interviews can be transcribed and survey results can be converted into digital data sets that can be analyzed using statistical measures.

10. *Analysis and interpretation of the data:* Here, the results of the investigation are evaluated in a very concrete way, taking into account the initial research question. The data are analyzed and prepared accordingly (graphically) for a presentation.

11. *Presentation of research results:* In the final step, the results are presented. Here, recommendations for possible new products or adjustments to the existing portfolio can already be made on the basis of the information found.

With the knowledge gained from market observation, you can understand your target market much better and adapt your products to the specific requirements and wishes. To do this, your next step should be to define an ideal company that is one hundred percent like your target customer. Describe what requirements and challenges the company has now and in the near future and work out how your products can optimally support this customer. Further define what an ideal contact person in the company looks like. After that, you can tailor your sales messages to best fit. Your sales team can then use the ideal customer description and match it with existing customer lists to find potential buyers. Potential new customers can also be matched with this profile right away.

In addition to market observation in the target market, the so-called mega trends should always be kept in mind. These are global trends that have an impact on all industries. Although these trends do not change as frequently as individual market trends, the current mega-trends should be known and the global impact on one's own business should be permanently monitored. For example, the topics of sustainability and CO_2 reduction are current mega-trends that cut across all industries and nations. A company from the automotive industry, for example, can narrow down this trend to its own industry in a first step and analyze what effects the trend will have in the short, medium, and long term. Then, in a next step, the effects on the own company can be analyzed. In a final step, new business models, products, and services can then be developed that are aimed precisely at this trend. In this case, for example, this would be a consistent orientation of production in the direction of electric vehicles, energy-saving optimization of production, and the creation of new mobility services as an alternative to owning one's own car.

Be aware that the task of market observation is never complete and that all insights gained from the data are only snapshots. Business Development should therefore permanently try to have an impression of the current and future market situation. This is the only way to optimally support and develop the business.

In the following, the Gartner Hype Cycle is presented as a special tool that you can use as part of your market observation.

5.1.1   Gartner Hype Cycle

New business models and production techniques are nowadays based in many parts on digital technology. Digitalization is now influencing almost all areas. It is therefore extremely important for Business Development to have a good overview of current and future technological developments and trends. Not only the technology as such, but also the effects on the own industry and the own offers must be analyzed and understood. Only then can one optimize one's own business accordingly and plan future business sensibly. By far not every technological trend is really meaningful or sustainable and influential. Thus, each trend must be examined to determine if and when it will really achieve traction in the economy and what influences it could have on one's own business. Thus, a tool is needed that supports the early assessment of new technologies and helps to prevent wrong decisions and bad investments.

The market research company Gartner developed the Gartner Hype Cycle for this purpose a few years ago (cf. [14]). Do not be confused by this, because the Hype Cycle is not a cycle in the true sense of the word. Rather, Gartner evaluates selected technological topics in different areas once a year and rates them based on two criteria:

- **Y-axis:** This axis assesses how high the expectations are for the new technology and how much attention a given topic receives at the time of study. To this end, market research is used to examine how much a given topic is talked about and discussed (on- and offline), how much science is devoted to a topic, and the extent to which early adaptation of a topic can be observed on the market.

- *X-axis:* Time is considered on this axis. It evaluates how long a given subject can be observed.

Gartner has used its experience from years of market observation to identify a sequence of five critical phases that every new technology goes through. These phases are described in detail below. Figure 5.1 shows the Gartner Hype Cycle graphically.

1. ***Technological Trigger:*** The first phase of the Hype Cycle describes the point of introduction of a new technology. Usually there is a rudimentary idea at this point, or a very early prototype. However, this is often sufficient for people with an affinity for technology to show initial interest at an early stage and for the first venture capital to be raised. At this point, the technology is not yet known to the masses.
2. ***Peak of Inflated Expectations:*** In the second phase, the hype has reached its peak. The topic is on everyone's lips and is celebrated in all media as "the next big thing". At this point, many people and companies from a wide variety of sectors are looking into the topic and a lot of money is being spent on a technology with an uncertain outcome. There is a gold-rush atmosphere.
3. ***Trough of Disillusionment:*** In the next phase, it slowly becomes apparent what the technology can really do and whether it was worth the hype. Here it is realized that many claims are not true or were far too benevolent and that they cannot be implemented in

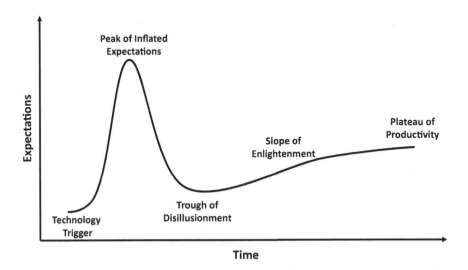

Fig. 5.1 The Gartner Hype Cycle

reality. Early investors have often lost a lot of money to date and begin to demonize the technology.

4. *Slope of Enlightenment:* This is the phase where the wheat is separated from the chaff. Technologies that have real potential start to really build traction here and initial implementations come to market. Investment picks up in this phase and a broader mass of companies begin to look at the technology and its impact on their own business.

5. *Plateau of Productivity:* In the last phase, the technology has finally gained acceptance and reached the mass market. The technology has become manageable, has been used many times in a wide variety of products and services, and has achieved widespread acceptance in the marketplace.

Each element is evaluated in terms of when it will truly become market relevant, how many more years it will take to do so, and whether it will fail early on and thus never reach the productivity phase.

The Gartner Hype Cycle is an important tool for Business Development to evaluate and classify current and future trends. It helps to quickly gain a broad overview of current technologies and to assess their relevance to one's own business.

The tool does not reflect any absolute truths and has no scientific claim. Nevertheless, it has become accepted as the "quasistandard" for evaluating new technologies and their market relevance. Business Development Managers should review the Hype Cycles relevant to their industry at least once a year and evaluate their possible impact on their own business. This may reveal approaches for optimizing one's own business by integrating a new technology, or it may result in completely new business models by picking up on a new technology at an early stage.

5.2   Market Segmentation

After a detailed market analysis has been drawn up and the target market has been defined, Business Development can be used to segment the market in the next step. Here, the target market is broken down into subsets using previously defined criteria. Possible criteria for market segments are, for example,

- Gender
- Age Group
- Level of education
- Purchasing power
- Number of employees
- Company sales

- Legal form
- Industry
- Headquarters

In the next step, it is then possible to examine exactly which segments are particularly suitable for the product. For this, the needs of the respective customers in a given segment must be precisely analyzed and compared with the solution offered. When examining a market segment in which a product of its own is already being sold, the analysis should determine the level of penetration of this segment and the exact sales figures. In addition, all market entrants who also serve this segment should be covered and their respective offers closely scrutinized in order to develop, in the next step, a sales message different from that of the competitors and highlighting your own benefits.

When segmenting the target market, pay attention to selective criteria. Otherwise, you will get segments whose elements (your target customers) are not well defined. This makes it more difficult to create a targeted sales message later. Then rate which of the found segments are particularly interesting for you. It would be possible to make an assessment based on the estimated sales volume, the number of target customers in the segment, the competitor situation or the previous market penetration. You can perform a classic ABC analysis by sorting the individual segments in descending order according to the criterion you have defined. This gives you a good classification of the target market.

The more accurately you perform this analysis, the sharper the individual segments are from each other. Search for the smallest possible and most promising number of target segments in which you want to place the product. You may even choose only the segment with the greatest potential. This is very advantageous because you can analyze the needs of the target customers in this segment very precisely and then generate a very spotty sales message. Avoid the watering can principle, in which the sales message is very unspecifically formulated and given to a very broad mass. This is in most cases not very effective and wastes marketing budgets.

After you have found and precisely analyzed your target segment, Business Development can generate highly targeted sales messages together with marketing. These can then be adapted to the requirements of the segment. Possible adaptations of your speech can take into account the following points:

- Current situation of target customers
- Current needs of target customers
- Current issues of target customers
- Current challenges of target customers
- Current bottlenecks of target customers
- Preferred approach to target customers
- Preferred communication channels of the target customers

Once you have found your target customer' segment and created a sales message that is precisely tailored to the specific needs of the customer, you should also examine the market for its risks. The following chapter will discuss this topic in more detail.

5.3 Risk Analysis

Entering a new market is both a chance and a risk. You should always be aware of that. Therefore, it is a very important task of Business Development when planning a new market entry or changing a business model to examine both sides in detail. New markets always represent a new situation that should be illuminated from all angles. Only then can later surprises be avoided. In fact, the introduction of a new product or service can have legal implications, possible lawsuits can have financial implications, business spies could steal important plans, data breaches can be very damaging, patent infringement can lead to high fines, and all of this can lead to an unpredictable image damage.

The following section describes how you can approach a risk analysis in a structured way and identify potential risks at an early stage and possibly even avert them. For this purpose, two methods have prevailed. These are the SWOT analysis and the STEP analysis. The results of the two analyzes together give a good idea of the chances, opportunities, and potential dangers for a business under investigation and should be the starting point for strategic decisions for or against a business.

Note that a detailed risk analysis should be performed at the beginning of an action or other strategic decisions through Business Development. The identified risks should then be managed in a targeted manner. This means that attempts should be made to initially avoid potential risks, or at least to minimize their probability of occurrence. Keep in mind, however, that this is not a one-off action, but a risk assessment should be carried out on an ongoing basis as the risk factors may change over time.

To assess the impact of a risk, you can multiply the estimated probability of occurrence by the estimated damage. The values obtained in this way can be sorted in descending order and then decide for which risks you want to counteract actively and which risks you perceive, but do not want to further mitigate (at the moment).

In the following, the two best-known analysis tools are presented in detail.

5.3.1 SWOT Analysis

The SWOT analysis is used in many companies as the standard tool for strategic planning of product or even whole company strategies. It should be mastered by every Business Development Manager. The acronym stands for Strengths, Weaknesses, Opportunities, and Threats. This evaluates the four most important influences on a business. In the following the individual points are briefly explained (see [20]):

- *Strengths:* Here you evaluate the individual strengths of your company, the respective area of a company or a product. What distinguishes the product? What are the unique selling points? How do you differentiate yourself from market entrants? How does it support your customers? What problems does it solve? Where are other strengths?
- *Weaknesses:* In this section you evaluate the weaknesses. Where are known weaknesses, for example, of a product? Where are market entrants better? Where do you not meet the demands of your customers? Are not all (safety) regulations or standards complied with? Is your product too little known in the market? What are other weaknesses?
- *Opportunities:* Every market offers opportunities that you should take advantage of. But you have to recognize them, evaluate them, and then make targeted use of them. Is there perhaps a cyclical upturn? Can you borrow cheap money for an important investment? Have you found a lucrative gap in the market? Can you enter a foreign market? Have economic or legal requirements changed? What else is there for opportunities?
- *Threats:* Of course every market has its dangers. You should know these even better than your chances, as it can have potentially worse consequences to overlook a danger than to miss a chance. Which legal or economic conditions could change? Do customers have permanent demand for your products? Is the market big enough? Are there any other competitors with better terms? Can all resources required for production be procured permanently on the same terms? Are the markets shifting? Could there be privacy issues or IT security issues? Can there be image damage? Are there any other risks?

After examining all four areas in detail, you can merge the results. The results of a SWOT analysis are usually compared in a graph with four quadrants. Here, the mutual influences are easy to read. In Fig. 5.2, a SWOT matrix is graphically displayed. Summarize the key points of the four areas. Describe how you can use your strengths and circumvent your weaknesses to seize the opportunities and counteract the dangers.

5.3.2 STEP Analysis

The STEP analysis, or also PEST analysis, limits the analysis of the more general SMOT analysis to the following macroeconomic topics (see [10]):

- *Sociocultural Change:* Here, the sociocultural aspects are gathered for a given market. These may be demographic data such as population growth and lifestyle, income distributions, educational attainment, social values, and standards.
- *Technological Change:* This is where the technical aspects that can impact on market entry are compiled. For example, these may include the current state of research, product life cycles, engineering developments, or research subsidies.

Fig. 5.2 The SWOT Analysis

- *Economic Change:* Here, the economic aspects of a given market are aggregated. These may include monetary effects such as current interest rates, exchange rates, and interest rates, but also current unemployment rates, possible economic cycles and resource availability.
- *Political Change:* It brings together political aspects that can have impacts on the product or marketplace. This may include the current political situation and stability in the country of destination, specific legislation affecting the product or market entry, tax implications, potential trade embargoes, security policies, or government subsidies.

After analysis, the effects found are usually displayed in a graphic. Figure 5.3 shows such a graphic.

There is also an extension to the classic STEP / PEST analysis. It is abbreviated to PESTLE, where the L stands for Legal and examines specific legal aspects and the E stands for Environment and examines ecological aspects.

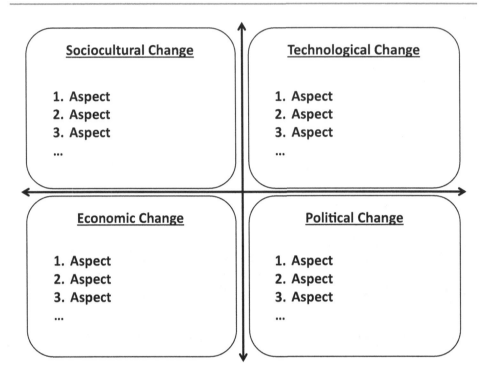

Fig. 5.3 The STEP Analysis

5.4   Internationalization

It can also be an object of Business Development to internationalize existing products or services. There are many points to consider, which are explained below.

The internationalization of products is a very complex task, as it is not enough simply to offer an existing product in another country. Many topics have to be clarified in advance. This begins with an extensive market observation (see Sect. 5.1). This will first clarify in which country or, better still, on which continent a market entry makes sense at all. Maybe some countries or even a whole continent can be excluded immediately. This should also take into account existing trade embargoes. Maybe it makes sense to address the immediate neighboring countries first. Here the cultural and technological differences are not so big. Also, currency differences and the general economic loading play a big role. For example, proper timing may be very important for entering the market abroad as political or legal conditions often change. All these aspects have to be included in the market analysis. So first define a destination country and then work out what the demand in that country looks like for your product and what the sales potential is. Also note that you may position yourself against market companions from the destination country. Compare exactly how you need to place your product to generate added value.

Many products are very specific to a country-specific market segment. Internationalization often requires adaptation to the requirements of the destination country. These requirements may be of a legal nature, certain safety regulations may apply or certain technical standards must be complied with. This requires a lot of specific know-how. For example, just think about the different power systems worldwide. If you want to sell a product that requires power for operation, you need to clarify what voltages are available in the destination country, which connector system to use, which standards and safety regulations to follow, and whether this is compatible with your product at all or larger adjustments would be necessary. It is best to consult a specialist who can help you prepare for a market launch. For example, different legal systems, other tax systems, other import and customs systems, and many other requirements, which are highly dependent on the products or services, apply in all countries. All these things have to be clarified in advance in a clear and legally secure manner. For example, in the United Arab Emirates, you may only do business if you have a local business sponsor who vouches for you to the authorities.

In other countries, there is often a very different social and cultural environment. This can have a direct or indirect impact on your offer or product. Furthermore, a completely different price structure may exist in the destination country. You should then check whether a distribution in this country is even lucrative for you. If you think about international sales, it can often make sense, at least in the beginning, to think about indirect distribution with local distributors. This has many advantages as you do not have to build up staff on-site, or salespeople may need to send expensive business trips. In addition, the partner knows the country, the specifications and other conditions very well and may be able to better position your product in the market. When the partnership starts successfully and your products find the desired sales, you can still think about your own sales at a later date.

If you are not just thinking about international distribution, but about relocating production (at least in part) abroad, you will need to consider other things. Some of them have already been described in the Sect. 4.4 in the sections on Near- and Offshoring. Take note of the supply chains, the deliverability of raw materials and local and international logistics chains. Remember also that in other countries the mentality of the employees is often quite different and the pay structure can be completely different. In international production, legal and tax requirements play an even stronger role than in pure distribution. Here you should definitely seek legal assistance from a specialist.

When planning internationalization, however, you should always keep in mind that stepping into a new country will give you many chances and opportunities. But there are also many risks that you should describe in advance as accurately as possible in order to avoid them as much as possible. Again, a SWOT analysis can help here (see Sect. 5.3.1). When creating the business plan (see Sect. 2.5.4), be aware that business abroad may be slower than you would like. Keep your expectations and above all the expectations of the management realistic and plan together with the controlling a realistic business case.

Conclusion for Daily Business

- An important task of Business Development is the permanent market observation. All the relevant market activities, technological and sociological trends and the competitive situation are closely examined in order to draw conclusions for the adjustment of your own business.
- Segment your target market as accurately as possible. Use clear criteria to obtain segments that are as non-overlapping as possible. This helps you to work out specific customer needs more precisely and to define products and sales messages that are tailored to the respective segment in the next step.
- Before you develop a new product or change an existing product or business model, you should perform a detailed risk analysis. This helps you to identify risks at an early stage, which can then be avoided or at least mitigated. Note that risk analysis is a permanent task because risk scenarios can change quickly.
- In the event of possible internationalization, keep in mind that other political, technical, and cultural factors play a role in each country. Inform yourself early and extensively about possible effects on your business. Get the best external support or partners who already have experience in your new target market.

Market Cultivation Strategy

Abstract

The market cultivation strategy is at the heart of Business Development. This is because apart from the actual development of new products and services in Business Development, it is all about improving existing products, repositioning them on the market (or in new markets), or optimizing existing business models and new ones Adapt conditions to increase overall product success. There are various parameters that Business Development can work on to boost product sales. An important point is the price model. It must be adapted to the requirements of the customer and at the same time adjusted in such a way that a maximum return can be achieved. On the one hand, the sales concept can be used to optimize the message to customers and, on the other, to address a broader or even an international market through the integration of new sales channels. To support their own sales, partners who also sell their own products can also be brought on board. The products can simply be resold or refined with additional products or services. Here too, Business Development can increase sales with a targeted partner strategy. The marketing strategy is rounded off by targeted marketing, which helps translate the product information into incentives to buy and position the sales messages in a wide range of channels. In addition, Business Development can also support sales enablements. Especially in the beginning, after a product change or after the introduction of a new product, employees from Business Development accompany the sales staff in concrete customer situations. The aim of the market cultivation strategy is to position the product optimally with a market-driven pricing model, in a well-defined market, via well-defined and controlled sales and marketing channels. The individual concepts are presented below.

© Springer Fachmedien Wiesbaden GmbH, part of Springer Nature 2023   113
A. Kohne, *Business Development*,
https://doi.org/10.1007/978-3-658-38844-7_6

6.1   Pricing

Once the new product or service has been established, a pricing model must be found
for distribution. There are different pricing models that are in many areas depending on
the product or service. The pricing should be carried out in agreement between the sales,
the management, production, and Business Development. Basically, Business Development
should develop a pricing concept that describes how and in which periods money is earned
with the product. The amount of the price should not matter at first. Please note that the choice
of the pricing model has a direct impact on your company's sales mix. In case of doubt,
there are also guidelines from the management, which type of sales should be increased in
the future, or which type of sales should be added. Since there are many different pricing
options, only the best known will be presented below.

Pricing Models:

- *Purchase Price:* The classic among the pricing models is certainly the simple purchase
  price. It is often used for products sold either directly to end customers or to middlemen.
  There is still a distinction between a single price and a group price. In the second case,
  discounts are often granted when purchasing a larger number of products. Often the
  discounts increase with the number of products. This increase is then planned in so-
  called discount scales.
  If the product is a major purchase, often a purchase contract is set up, which regulates,
  among other things, the payment arrangements. For large amounts, for example, an
  installment can be offered.
- *License:* The license is also a widely used pricing model. A limited or unrestricted right
  to use a product is transferred to the licensee for a certain period of time. For example,
  this model is often used in commercial software.
- *Service by Expense:* If you sell services, you can choose between two different pricing
  models. In the first model, the service will be charged according to effort. You owe the
  customer no result. Although fixed goals or milestones are often defined by the customer
  as contractually expected, these are processed within the previously agreed time. If a goal
  cannot be achieved, this must be remedied by another commission from the customer.
  Such contracts are also called "time and material contracts because they are settled
  according to the time and material used.
- *Fixed Price Service* The second model for selling services is the so-called service contract. In doing so, you owe the customer a product or result accepted by the customer under
  previously agreed criteria. Since, unlike the services, you have to sell a completed project
  at a cost, where you have to plan all internal and external expenses in advance, a risk
  premium is often added to the final price in order to compensate for any miscalculations.
- *Lend:* You can also lend your products. In doing so, you provide the customer with the
  product for a defined period of time and charge a rental fee. This fee is to be calculated

so that the product amortized over a period to be defined, the wear and possibly the maintenance and service are included and of course a total profit.

- *Leasing* You can also rent or offer the product through a lease contract. Similar to lending, you provide the product for a contracted period of time and charge a rent or lease fee (for example, monthly). In many cases, the customer is offered to take over the product at a previously fixed price after the end of the contract after expiry of a contractually agreed period.
- *Subsidy:* Another pricing model is subsidizing. Hereby, the core product is purposely sold below the actually calculated final price in order to quickly build up a larger customer base. The difference to the actual price is then earned through additional options in the later customer relationship. Thus, this model pays off only after a certain time. Classic examples of such a pricing model are the partly heavily subsidized mobile devices that are sold on conclusion of a mobile phone contract, or the game consoles of the manufacturers Sony and Microsoft. Here, the consoles are sold at a bargain price and profits are made via additional services and license participations in the games.
- *On-Demand/Pay-as-you-go:* This price model is mainly used in the last few years The field of cloud computing and video streaming has become fashionable. Instead of paying a license fee, or a fixed monthly price, this will be charged according to real consumption. This allows the customer to use the product very flexibly, since the usage is only billed when it really takes place. This can save costs, because the product no longer has to be purchased completely, but it is used as needed and billed. Thus, the costs for the customer shift from CAPEX to OPEX.

  To be able to offer such a model, the provision and production must be extremely flexible and there may be no or hardly no jump-fixed costs. Thus, this model can be found especially in IT-based systems in which many users can share a system, without resulting in large cost differences for the operator with fluctuating numbers of users. An on-demand model has to be planned very precisely so that it pays off permanently after a certain number of users. Thus, it is also clear that such a model generates losses at the beginning. This must necessarily be planned with and communicated accordingly, since otherwise it can come to problems with the management.
- *Freemium:* The latest pricing model currently heavily used by online services is called Freemium. This is an artificial word that was generated from the two English words "free" and "premium" in the sense of added value (see [48]). The basic idea of this model is that a basic service or product is offered free of charge and additional services or functions are charged for. For example, many e-mail providers offer the basic service for free. For additional storage space or multiple email addresses will then be due a monthly amount. This business model has also become established in the computer games industry. Here is then spoken of "Free-to-play". The aim of this model is to quickly build a broad and potentially international customer base through the free basic service, which can then be served with additional services.

Which model is best for your specific case, of course, must be decided individually. There is no right or wrong and it is not possible to say which overall is the best pricing model. Choose the one that best suits you and your product. In case of doubt, price models can of course also be adjusted later. But always make sure that the changes are not detrimental to the existing customers. This could potentially cause you to lose them.

6.2   Sales Concept

Business Development usually also supports the definition of the sales concept. In doing so, the brand or product message is created in such a way that it can be made available in the most appropriate way for the target customer and reaches the customer in an appropriate manner. This means that a good sales concept is geared to the needs of the customer. The central question is: How would the customer be addressed and what information does he need to make a purchase decision?

The sales concept is usually created together with the sales department. Often, the marketing department also supports the formulation and the design of the sales messages. When creating the sales concept, the results of the market observation are used to create the sales message in a targeted manner (see Sect. 5.1). Of course, the results of the definition of the target customer and the target customer segment also play a major role (see Sect. 5.2). Furthermore, it must be known who the contact person the customer is in order to be able to adapt the messages to concrete needs. In addition, the pricing (see Sect. 6.1) and the actual product description is needed to create a meaningful message. The product description should be designed so that, on the one hand, the specific needs of the customer are precisely recorded and described. On the other hand, the benefits of the product and the way in which it supports the customer, how to solve a specific problem or how to satisfy a need should be described. It may be that different messages have to be created for different target customers in different segments because they have different requirements for the product. Create the right message for each channel and for each target customer or segment, detailing the unique selling proposition of the product.

In the next step, it will then be determined which distribution channels are most meaningful for the marketing. At first, a distinction is made between direct sales and indirect sales. In direct sales, the sales staff of your company sells the product itself and directly to the end customer. In an indirect distribution, you have intermediaries between yourself and your end customers. These can be, for example, wholesalers who then sell the products to end users. But it is also possible to have a multi-layered model with several intermediaries. Depending on your product, there are also other distribution options. Of course, the choice of the right distribution channel also depends heavily on whether it is a product or a service. Services are usually sold directly or through distribution partners (see Sect. 6.3); rarely through a multi-stage sales process with intermediaries. In addition, you can also use freelance agents or reach your customers via (internal or external) telephone acquisition. In recent years, the online sales has become more prevalent. Here you have (almost) no direct customer contact anymore, but your customers order their products directly through a webshop or through a large online distribution platform. Always choose the best form of sales contact for your customers. It is quite possible to combine several distribution channels. For example, through the combination of direct sales and an online shop you can reach your customers on the one hand very simply and on the other hand offer a platform that is even internationally available and thus promises a wide distribution and visibility.

6.3 Partner Concept

Partners are very important in today's business life. A well-structured partner landscape can inspire the business and open up many more sales channels. In order to select the right partners and to steer them correctly, a good partner concept is needed. The advantage of partners is that you can concentrate on your strengths and look for partners who will provide you with the best possible support. But the partners must be chosen carefully. Business Development can help here because partnerships are often closed in a specific business area. Thus, a fundamental partner strategy should first be developed by Business Development, which describes why and in which areas what partners are being sought. Furthermore, you need a sophisticated partner management. It defines how to deal with the various active partners. In doing so, you should define a well-defined lifecycle from partner onboarding, through partner engagement, through partnership, to partnership termination. Especially the last step is very important, because it is often forgotten. As a result, many partnerships are often accumulated over the years, which both sides can no longer live up to. Partnerships that only exist on paper do not bring anything to any side and should be terminated. It does not help anyone to boast with as many partnerships as possible. Choose a small number of partners, but you can work with them strategically. Work out a corresponding partner contract, which defines all key parameters that are important to you, from confidentiality obligations and possible discount scales for sales through to production planning. Also, remember to work with your partner to develop a sales plan in which you both agree on a common revenue for a specific period of time. Compliance with these contracts must then be controlled at runtime. For this purpose, you best build up your own partner management. Of course, this is worthwhile only from a certain size or from a certain number of partners. In some cases, it pays off to hire an employee for partner management. Maybe only for the management of a strategically important partner.

Newly acquired partners must first be provided with all relevant information. This is best defined by a kind of onboarding process for new partners. In doing so, the partner receives all the relevant information and a permanent contact person in your company, who is the first instance for all questions.

Step by step build up a whole network of partners for the different areas. In this context, one often speaks of a so-called partner ecosystem.

In the following, the most important types of partnerships are briefly explained:

- *Distributors* Distributors help you bring your products and services to a wider audience. Partners can either sell their products directly or incorporate them into their products and solutions. Thus, you also reach customers who are not yet part of your direct customers. This step also allows for cross-selling, where you can selectively sell additional products to the new customers.

  Furthermore, distribution partners can also help you with internationalization. If, for example, you want to sell your products abroad, then before you set up your own branch office in the target country or send in your own sales staff, you can search for local partners who sell your product abroad (see Sect. 5.4).

- *Technology Partner:* Technology partners help in production with special know-how or machines. They may also supply software components or special products that can be used in customer projects. These partners are very important as the business would be very costly or even impossible without them. This is because not every company can or wants to re-develop every technology they need. This can be done by establishing strategic partnerships, that help both sides to generate more business.

- *Suppliers:* Fixed partnerships can also be negotiated with suppliers. Here, for example, exclusive rights can be granted in return for favorable conditions. This ensures a low purchase price for the suppliers and secures the supplier to the other fixed purchase quantities. Thus both sides win.

- *Financial Partner:* Financial partners are also very important because a company can only work if the necessary financial resources are available. In order to secure the continued existence of a company, it should permanently rely on further development. In order to finance this development, it is often necessary to raise money externally. Good partnerships pay off here.

6.4   Marketing Concept

After discussing market observation and customer segment analysis (see Sects. 5.1 and 5.2) in detail in the last chapters, the sales and pricing concept were also explained (see Sects. 6.1 and 6.2), the results from these parts can now be merged into the Marketing Concept. The Marketing Concept is usually created by the marketing department. But here, too, Business Development can support, because it is a good sparring partner, who knows a lot about the product and the target customers. The marketing concept accompanies and supports the Sales Concept.

In the following, the structure of a Marketing Concept is presented in seven steps:

1. *Status Quo Analysis* First, do an analysis of the status quo. Where are you standing? Where do your customers stand? What does the current market situation look like? What

current influences could affect your product (political, economic, social influences)? Also use the results from the risk analysis (see Sect. 5.3). What risks do you see and more importantly, how can you handle or minimize them? Also find out how your target customers want to be addressed and what kind of relationship they want.

Make sure that you have a complete picture of the current situation, so that your marketing concept is not based on wrong assumptions or wrong assessments. In this phase, also define the available budget.

2. *Marketing Goals* The next step is to define the goals of the marketing concept. From the start, make sure that your concept fits into the corporate concept as seamlessly as possible. Clarify the basic orientation at this point: What should be achieved through the marketing concept? Do you want to inform customers? Do you want to attract attention? Do you want to sensitize the customers? Above all, define measurable goals that you want to achieve with the concept. Should the number of active customers be increased? If so, how many new customers should be won in which period? How big should your market share be after which period? How many customers in your target segment should know your product after what period of time?

3. *Marketing Strategy:* In this step, you define your strategy for the new product. Clarify how you want to be perceived as a company. What does the product stand for and what does your company stand for? Also analyze how your competitors are moving in the target market. Which products already exist and how do your competitors advertise? In the strategy, you also commit yourself to the specific target segments in order to be able to position your marketing messages in a targeted manner. Also here the product to be advertised is exactly defined and described. Your marketing efforts may also be accompanied by an internal marketing campaign. This makes sense in many situations. This ensures that internal employees are also familiar with and can report on their products and innovations. Also note that you may need to define different strategies for different markets. Keep in mind what kind of customers you are planning your business with. If you sell your products to companies, your business is referred to as B2B (Business to Business). Working with government agencies, this type of business is referred to as B2G and certainly requires a different marketing strategy than selling directly to end-users B2C (Business to Consumer).

4. *Marketing Tools:* The next step is to define the tools that will be used to implement the marketing strategy you have just defined. Here the "4Ps" of marketing are often used. These are the well-known marketing tools "Product, Place, Price & Promotion" (see [30]):

   – *Product:* This is a detailed description of the product. What is it? How does it look like? What is its unique selling point (the USP)? What variants are there? What problems does it solve? What is included? What does the customer get after the purchase? How can the product be used?

- *Place:* There are two different aspects of distribution or distribution policy. On the one hand, there is the logistical aspect that describes how, for example, topics such as storage and production are dealt with, and, on the other hand, there are acquisition aspects that are defined with the help of the sales concept (see Sect. 6.2).
- *Price* Pricing must be tailored to the product and the target customer segments. Here, on the one hand, the amount of the product price is determined and on the other hand, in which way the customers pay for the product (see Sect. 6.1).
- *Promotion:* This defines the actual marketing concept. How are the target customers reached? What message needs to be conveyed? In which ways is the product advertised?

When defining marketing tools, be aware that you may need different messages for different customer segments or even different marketing channels. However, always remember to define the simplest messages that immediately add value to the customer. Examples of marketing tools include the following:

- Classic print/print advertising in daily newspapers, magazines
- Online advertising with the help of advertising banners
- Content marketing with reports
- Television advertising
- Radio advertising
- Fair appearances and other events (external or self-organized)
- Roadshows
- (Exclusive) Customer events
- Cold-calling campaigns
- E-mail (advertising or newsletter)
- SMS advertising
- Social media advertising

5. *Marketing Mix:* In this step, the previously defined tools are merged into an integral concept. It should be ensured that the different marketing activities in the different channels are coordinated and synchronized with each other. This avoids communication problems and also makes it easier to monitor the planned goals. At this point, make sure that the activities planned here are integrated into the company-wide brand strategy. Check in defined time periods whether the Marketing Mix chosen at the beginning is still suitable and change it if necessary.

6. *Realization of the marketing concept:* In this step, the previously planned marketing concept is implemented. Thus, the previously defined marketing messages are disseminated via the selected channels. Make sure that you always include a "Call to Action" at the end of any activity. By this is meant that at the end of each advertisement, a call should be positioned to the customer, who calls him to the next step. For this purpose, offer an e-mail address or a hotline for special questions, or offer to send further information by post or even send a sales representative. This ensures that interested customers respond quickly and come to you.

7. ***Controlling:*** In the last step you control the results of the marketing activities. Was the budget completely used up? Could enough customers be reached? Were the planned sales figures reached? Have enough sales appointments been generated? Did enough participants come to the fair? Has the number of new customers increased as planned? Also check here if further measures are necessary and if perhaps something could be improved at the next planning round. This will help you get better with each pass and better reach the previously defined goals.

In order to more easily approach the topic of marketing, there is a very simple and visual approach. It was developed by a company called XPLANE and is called "Customer Empathy Map" (see [49]). It uses a simple graphic and an exemplary customer to analyze how the customer feels, what he thinks, and what he exactly wants. For this purpose, the following points are examined:

Points of the Customer Empathy Map (see Fig. 6.1):

- ***Listen:*** What does the customer hear? From whom does he hear it? What influences him? How is he influenced by it?

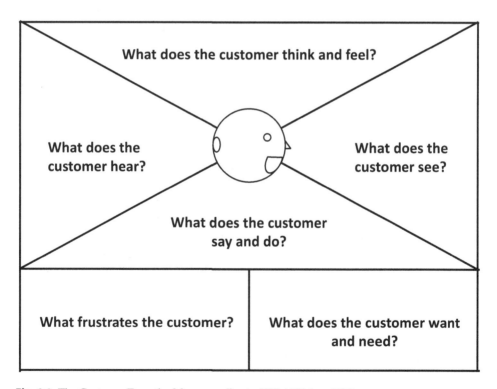

Fig. 6.1 The Customer Empathy Map according to XPLANE (see [49])

- *Think and feel:* What does the customer think? What does the customer feel? What are his hopes? What are his worries? What are his challenges? What are his professional and private goals?
- *See:* What does the customer see? Where does the customer see this? What does he perceive? How does he see the market? How does he/his company see himself? How does he see his environment? What else does he see?
- *Say and do:* What does the customer say? How does he say it? To whom does he say it? What is the customer doing? Where does the customer do it? With whom does he do it? In which situations does the customer say or do something?
- *Frustration:* What frustrates the customer? What are his fears? What are possible obstacles? What is blocking him? What bothers him? How can your product help reduce its frustration?
- *Desire:* What makes the customer happy? What are his goals? How can he achieve this? What are his wishes (private/professional)? How can your product lead him to a pleasure gain?

Completing this Empathy Map should take place in a workshop, involving people from different departments (for example, marketing, production, development, Business Development, and sales). The workshop should be led by a moderator to intervene in the expansive discussions and to remind all participants of the goal. The aim is to develop a good overview of the sensitivities of the target customers in order to create the best possible marketing concept.

6.4.1   Online Marketing

In addition to the classic sales channels, sales via the Internet have become an important instrument in sales in recent years. For many companies, so-called online marketing has even become the only sales channel. Business Development Managers should be at least fundamentally familiar with the techniques and processes and plan appropriate marketing measures together with the internal marketing and communications department.

The goal of online marketing is to generate new prospects (so-called leads) or customers in a fully or partially automated manner. In addition to a content strategy driven by marketing to increase sales with the help of social media, blogs, and newsletters, many companies have also established their own web store. The content relevant to the target groups should simultaneously inform and provide incentives to buy, which can be implemented immediately in the company's own web store.

Optimizing one's homepage and promoting one's products and services on major search engines are standard in online marketing. The formula applies: SEM = SEO + SEA.

- *SEM (Search Engine Marketing):* This includes all digital business activities to increase sales via the Internet with the help of search engines.
- *SEO (Search Engine Optimization):* This refers to the optimization of one's own home-page for better discoverability by the major search engines. There are many techniques and strategies that help to make a page more visible. The goal is to rank as high as possible in the organic search results without investing money for placement.
- *SEA (Search Engine Advertising):* The aim here is to use paid advertising to obtain a special advertising space in the respective search engines when searching for specific keywords or entire key phrases, which is then displayed exclusively to users alongside the organic results.

The concrete implementations are very individual and differ greatly depending on what is to be sold. Products are treated fundamentally differently than services. Furthermore, there are strong differences between B2B and B2C strategies. The price of a product can also have a strong influence on the chosen online marketing strategies. For example, when selling shoes, the goal is to reach a broad mass and focus on smooth ordering and returns processes. When selling high-priced watches or sports cars, the focus is on conveying exclusivity, luxury, and glamor. Accordingly, the marketing campaigns, the addresses and the advertisements used must also be implemented.

Overall, the goal of online marketing is to present one's own brand in a positive way, to be visible in the online market, and to bring additional target customers into the sales process. The term "sales funnel" has become established for this process. In this process, people from the target market are made aware of suitable offers through a process and then developed step by step into paying customers. Figure 6.2 shows a prototypical sales funnel, in which the funnel shape that gives it its name is clearly visible. In each of the funnel stages, the customer is provided with important information and incentives that lead him deeper into the funnel with each contact. Once they reach the end of the funnel, a prospect finally transforms into a paying customer. The individual stages of the funnel are described below:

1. *Unknown:* At the beginning, the person had no contact with the company. During a search on the Internet or through the insertion of suitable advertising, the person initially gets to know the corresponding offer.
2. *Awareness:* The person now focuses their attention on the product or service. At this stage, additional information must be offered (subliminally) to further increase attention. This can be done, for example, by displaying advertisements again with the help of retrageting. In this process, users on Internet pages can be "recognized" on the basis of cookies on other pages and be shown the same or similar advertising.
3. *Interest:* Now the person's interest has been piqued and he or she continues researching independently. At this point, the person should be directed to a central homepage or directly to a web store. Here, additional information can be offered in the form of text, images, and videos that further increase interest. At this point, videos are often used to

Fig.6.2 The Sales Funnel

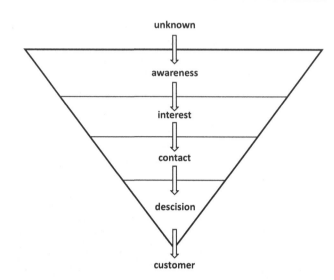

show the benefits of the product or service in a very concrete way. Furthermore, opinions of existing customers who have rated the offer positively are used here.

4. *Contact:* The next step is to bind the person closer to the company by offering newsletters or subscriptions to social media sites, for example. In this way, the prospect continuously receives precisely tailored information and interest continues to grow.

5. *Decision:* After further information has been obtained, the next step is the purchase decision. At this point, further purchase incentives can be set with limited-time special offers or additional offers (for example, free shipping) to persuade the prospective buyer to make a purchase.

6. *Customer:* In the final step, the prospect has decided to make a purchase and has successfully completed the ordering process. At this point, we speak of the so-called "conversion", as another prospect has been converted into a customer. Existing customers can be further tied to the company with additional information offers after the purchase and possibly be persuaded to purchase further offers

Online marketing is an effective strategy to get more prospects into the sales funnel. Of course, classic marketing and sales strategies can also be used in the offline area. The important thing is that the tools used to complement each other in a meaningful way and that the overall number of customers can be increased.

Another very successful method in the field of digital marketing is Social Selling.

6.4.2 Social Selling

Social Selling has become successfully established in recent years. Social selling covers all activities that the sales or Business Development departments carry out together with the marketing and communications departments in the area of social networks to increase sales.

In principle, Social Selling involves disseminating information about the company, its products and services, and other related areas in the social networks relevant to the company. The choice of the right networks is very important, as not every network is suitable for every company. So, together with specialists, it should be planned exactly which networks are to be used in order to be able to address the customers as precisely as possible. Otherwise, the efforts will go to waste and resources will be wasted unnecessarily. The aim of Social Selling is to build up a high level of customer loyalty in the social networks and, through strong proximity to customers and interested parties, to repeatedly provide targeted incentives to buy without merely distributing sales messages. The key to a successful Social Selling strategy is a good mix of different content that has a high relevance in the respective target customer segment. For example, technical information should be combined with background reports, interesting stories from the company with beautiful pictures, and sales messages with a personal touch.

In addition to a company page on the respective social media platform, employees from sales and Business Development in particular should be tasked with Social Selling, as it has been shown that content shared via personal profiles is much better received than content played out via a central company page.

All in all, Social Selling is another very effective sales tool that should be specifically planned into the sales strategy by Business Development in order to build up an additional source of potential new customers and optimum customer loyalty.

6.5 Sales Enablement

As part of creating a Market Cultivation Strategy, Sales Enablement should also be planned together with Business Development. This is understood to mean a targeted information campaign for sales, in which all information necessary for a successful sales process about a product is made available in a suitable form. Business Development should work closely with the product manager, the production department and above all the sales department.

With Sales Enablement, it is very important to generate the simplest messages sales can quickly absorb and reproduce to the customer. To achieve this, you should first define exactly what the unique selling point (USP) is. The USP summarizes the benefit that the customer has through the product or service and explains how to solve a specific problem or challenge for the customer or how to satisfy another need.

In the next step, create sales aids. These are written documents that you provide to distributors either in print or electronic form. You can do this, for example, during a sales meeting or make the documents centrally available via your intranet. The sales aids can describe in detail technical descriptions, product descriptions, variant descriptions, configuration options, USP messages, delivery conditions, terms, conditions and, if applicable, also the customer's obligation to cooperate. When creating the sales aids, make sure that the messages are intended for distribution. This means that you should not provide any deep technical documents, but much more from the customer's point of view, wondering which questions might arise in a sales pitch and who on the customer side in the sales process needs which information at what time to complete a successful sale.

In addition, you can also offer web and/or conference calls to help sales understand the new product. Similarly, it is possible for you to create a product video that can be used later in the sales process. You can even record sample customer conversations to help sales teams better prepare for customer discussions. If your company relies on telephone acquisition, you can also create telephone guides for customer meetings that provide specific procedures and preformulated sentences that help sales in a specific phone call to target the product.

Help your sales team with the question: who is the MAN (Money, Authority, Now)? Who besides a specific need has a suitable budget (money)? Who has the authority to decide on a purchase at the target customer? And who has the need now? The answers to these questions help in the sales process to identify the right contact persons at the target customers, so that they can be called or contacted in the next step with the appropriate sales approach.

Another important task of Business Development is pre-sales support or pre-sales consulting. This is understood as an accompaniment of the sales staff in the case of a specific customer situation by a specialist. Since Business Development helped develop the new product right from the beginning, there is of course a deep know-how available here. The aim of pre-sales consulting is that the specialist at the customer can also answer directly more in-depth questions and thus is an optimal supplement to the sales staff. After a certain period of time, the sales department should be able to answer even more in-depth questions and only use the pre-sales support if a customer expresses genuine buying interest. Otherwise, high personnel costs can arise at this point.

6.6   Networking

Companies need a reliable network or ecosystem of partners, companies, and individuals around them in order to be able to develop optimally in all directions. Building and maintaining an appropriate network are tasks that should not be underestimated. They require time and resources.

Business Development can take on this networking as a task. This includes networking with important people, organizations, partners, associations, up to (company or specialist) networks, etc. The goal is to find out the latest news, to stay up to date, and to exchange ideas. It is not the primary goal to immediately establish business connections. That would be a sales task. Rather, the goal is to be seen as a trustworthy contact person who is approachable and proactive. It is important to genuinely want to help, share knowledge, offer contacts, and provide third-party contacts. Networking should be an open and honest give and take. In this way, a resilient network is built up step by step, which can be reliably accessed when needed.

Networking today works online as well as offline. It is important to be actively represented in both worlds. Online, there are various business networks, social media, blogs, forums, and chat groups. There are a large number of very broad or highly specialized platforms and exchange opportunities to choose from as needed. Offline, there are various local, regional, national or even global events, trade fairs, industry meetings, clubs and associations, and other organizations.

You can also actively develop and run your own networking events. For example, you could offer regular after-hours events in a relaxed atmosphere or technology-focused "business breakfasts". For these events, you should draw on your internal marketing to help you plan, organize and execute.

The success of networking does not happen overnight; it takes time to build up an appropriate network. But once a contact person stands for a company, a topic or a technology in his network, he is the face associated with it. From this point on, he or she will automatically receive inquiries from the network without any further activity. These inquiries can be of a technical nature, for example. But there will definitely be sales-related inquiries, since he is known as a responsive problem solver in his field. From then on, the effort pays off and the network can grow.

Conclusion for Daily Business

- The Market Cultivation Strategy is at the heart of Business Development. It combines the concrete pricing, the sales, marketing, and partner concept. Here, Business Development provides the greatest added value, since here product know-how, industry knowledge, market observation, and salesmanship are needed to optimally place a given product in a target market.
- Find the best price for each product. You may also need different models for the same product in different markets or market segments. Set up here according to the wishes of your customers. Keep in mind that choosing the pricing model also influences your revenue mix.
- Create a concrete sales concept that defines exactly how your products reach their target customers via which channels. You may also include distributors here.
- Define unique parameters by means of which you can measure and control sales success with the help of controlling.
- Develop sales messages that are very carefully tailored to the needs of your customers. These messages can vary from customer segment to customer segment.
- Define a comprehensive marketing concept that should be tailored to each product. Make sure that you distribute your marketing messages purposefully only through

the channels through which your customers are reachable. Measure the result of your marketing activities and optimize your strategy permanently.

- Design a company-wide partner strategy. Partners help you focus on your core business and can significantly influence your success. Search for strategic partnerships and actively manage them. Only then can both sides benefit from it. Resolve unused or unsuccessful partnerships.
- Business Development should actively support sales at the customer, especially when launching a new product or changing a product or Business Model. This way, pre-sales consulting ensures that the customer's product value is explained quickly and clearly. However, at a later point in time sales should have built up so much product know-how that at least a first appointment can be carried out at a customer without any further support. For specific questions or closer interest, a product specialist should only be consulted in the second step.
- Build a resilient network and proactively get involved. This will give you additional visibility and more customer inquiries.

Case Study

7

Abstract

After presenting Business Development in detail in this book, a fictitious case study is presented below, which shows a complete run of the Business Development Process. Of course, not every step can be examined in detail here and not all decisions are presented with their alternatives, as this would not be effective. But the example illustrates how Business Development analyzes a given product and its market and then gradually introduces improvement and develops a new ecosystem around the product. As a result, new market potential can be raised and the product even positioned internationally.

7.1   Starting Situation

LSaS (Logistics Software and Services) is a medium-sized company with about 40 employees that has been operating successfully for more than 30 years. The most important product of the company is a software for the planning of warehouse logistics. The software has been further developed for many years and is currently being sold in version 6 and is a fixture in the market in this area. LSaS has more than 200 large and small logistics companies as customers who use the software to carry out their warehouse planning. Overall, the market is saturated, which means that there is no logistics company without warehouse planning software. It is therefore a mere predatory market in which prices have stagnated and even fallen in recent years. The provider market has consolidated considerably in the last ten years, leaving only about a handful of providers to fill this field.

For the most part, the company employs highly specialized software developers who have been developing this software for years, installing it with customers and supporting it during operation. They not only have special know-how for software development, but also have a deep understanding of warehouse logistics. The software is a classic Windows application

© Springer Fachmedien Wiesbaden GmbH, part of Springer Nature 2023
A. Kohne, *Business Development*,
https://doi.org/10.1007/978-3-658-38844-7_7

with a server running in the customer's data center and a user application installed on each PC.

The distribution of the software is carried out exclusively by LSaS personnel. The sales team consists of five people, who mainly serve the existing customers. New customers are to be won, for example, at special trade fairs and congresses; The software is also advertised on the internet. Turnover is achieved in total in three ways:

1. *License Sale:* The software is sold to a customer. For this, the customer pays a license price, which depends on the number of users. There is a base price for the software and then a user-based scale price, which provides for discounts as the number of users increases. The license price is due once during the sale.
2. *Maintenance:* Software customers may enter into a maintenance agreement when purchasing the software. Maintenance customers receive all product updates free of charge and can contact a free hotline if they have any problems. The maintenance price is 18% of the license costs and is due annually.
3. *Service:* LSaS offers an individual customizing of the software for its customers. Customizing is understood as the adaptation of software to the special wishes and requirements of customers that go beyond the standard range of functions. These are service projects of different duration, which bring very good sales, since only the employees of LSaS can adapt the software. So high daily rates can be achieved. Some large customers anticipate these efforts in advance and enter into master agreements on service quotas, which they can call up at a fixed price throughout the year.

Since the market is saturated, the company's sales have stagnated in recent years and there is no growth any more. Only a few new customers per year can be won, and these are usually small customers who generate little sales. The maintenance business is very lucrative and well predictable, but most of the revenue is used to cover ongoing staff costs. Maintenance revenues have become the main source of income in addition to customizing. Luckily, all customers have their own ideas about how the software should look and work for them, so that the customizing business is consistently well-performing and strong in sales.

At customer events, which are held every year for all existing customers, for a few years, the voices are growing louder, saying that the software was getting a bit old and that they wish something new.

The managing director of LSaS decides that something has to change in the company, because in the long run the rising costs eat up the dwindling sales. He decides to start a Business Development process in order to first analyze where potential growth areas could be and in a second step to develop and test a marketable idea. Since LSaS is a rather small company and cannot be charged with one person or even a whole team with the task of Business Development, the managing director decides that a virtual Business Development Team should be put together. Participants are beside the managing director the sales manager and the development manager. They all receive the task of Business Development in addition to their normal duties. Together they want to develop an idea that is innovative and that can increase the sales of LSaS in a future-proof way.

7.2   Business Development Process

In a first step, it is decided that a market analysis will be used to find out what the current market in the logistics segment looks like. For this purpose, the sales manager should talk to the existing customers and find out how satisfied they are with the current solution, what ideas and wishes they have and in addition to analyze the solutions of the competitors and find interesting concepts. The development manager should investigate which technologies are currently used in their particular industry and which technological trends are of importance in the IT sector as a whole. The CEO wants to find out about current business models and find out if there may be more up-to-date licensing options.

These are the results of market research:

1. *Customer requests:* In the conversations, the sales manager has often heard that customers would want a new, web-based solution with a modern user interface. Furthermore, the solution should be easier to use and, in the best case, be able to run on mobile devices such as smartphones and tablets. In addition, many customers complain that they have to operate the solution themselves. They say that their core business is logistics and they do not really want to afford a complete IT team that runs local IT. But many customers have concerns about a cloud solution because they consider data security as very critical. Since many logistics companies also work internationally, these customers also want to be able to use the software in different languages. This would reduce the training period in foreign locations.
   The competitor analysis shows that web-based solutions are becoming ever more prevalent and classic applications are increasingly being pushed out of the market.
   During the customer discussions, it was also found out that there are quite a few customers who would be interested in trying out a new solution together with the company LSaS and supporting the development process through early testing.
2. *Technological Possibilities:* While investigating the technological possibilities, the development manager found out that modern applications are developed either as a web application or directly as an app for smartphones or tablets, and secondly as an operating model "Software as a Service" (SaaS), which is derived from cloud computing, is on the rise. The application is no longer operated locally at the customer's site but in a large data center. In this data center, the software is operated on a uniform platform for all customers. This allows faster deployment and cheaper operation. Access to the application then takes place via the internet.

Both currents have many advantages. They can be made easier and cheaper for the customer, and they scale much more easily as customers grow. The only problem is that the company has no know-how on these topics at all.

3. *New Business Models:* In the analysis of modern business models in the field of software vendors, the manager encounters the new "pay-as-you-go" models. The customer no longer pays a fixed amount at the beginning of the contract period of a software use, but he pays on a (usually monthly) basis a fixed amount for the number of licenses used in each past accounting period. This enables demand-based billing, especially in areas with higher fluctuations.

Furthermore, the managing director sees more and more manufacturers concentrating on their core business and core competencies and looking for more strategic partners. Together, they form a strong ecosystem that helps each company focus on their respective strengths and grow their business together.

After compiling and discussing the results of the market analysis, the next step is brainstorming to develop ideas that link the lessons learned to the existing product. In the following, only the solution chosen in the end, which was developed by several iterations and intensive discussions and lively exchange with specialists, is presented:

The existing software will be maintained in the medium term and will be further developed. However, the development capacity is downgraded. Existing customers will continue to be provided with updates and service. An end to the software in three to five years is being considered. Until then, the software will run in cash cow mode (see Sect. 3.2).

At the same time, a new web-based version of the software is being developed. Examinations by a specialist have shown that a large part of existing software can be migrated to a new programming language with the help of a migration tool. This would preserve the entire business logic of the program and only a timely user interface has to be developed. For this two new specialists were hired. The developers freed by switching to the Chash-Cow mode will be trained to the new programming language and can now develop on both systems. The new software is planned from the outset so that it operates as a cloud service in a central data center. As a result, customers no longer have to install and operate the software locally. As a business model, a modern pay-as-you-go model was designed, which allows customers to flexibly buy or return new licenses on a monthly basis. For this, a completely new contract must be drafted and the billing and controlling must be adjusted accordingly, since the payment terms have changed. In addition, a pay-as-you-go model must be planned differently than a classic license business. Initially, a set-up fee is charged for new customers and existing customers can be migrated to the new solution in a small project. The new solution should first be operated in question mark mode, with the possibility of turning into a star (see Sect. 3.2).

Once the technology issue has been clarified and SaaS has been defined as a business model, it remains to decide what the operation of the solution might look like. For this purpose, different scenarios were again designed. They ranged from building their own data center, renting data center services, to using cloud services. However, there were always two problems with all these ideas: Firstly, the company did not have the necessary know-how to set up and operate such a solution, and secondly, the initial costs for setting up a data center and operating team were very high. Therefore, the manager introduced the idea that just in this case, a partner could be involved. Also this idea was discussed again in several rounds, before first discussions with potential partners were led. In the end, a partner was found that operates its own data centers. Furthermore, the partner has extensive experience in the operation of cloud software and has a web-based shop, through which he sells the solutions operated by him worldwide. After several discussions with the partner about the financial arrangement of the partnership, a so-called revenue-share model could be agreed as part of the definition of the Market Cultivation Strategy. In doing so, LSaS does not pay the partner for the provision of the data center services, but instead allocates all the revenue generated by customers according to a contractually agreed key. In this specific case, it was agreed that 60% of the monthly turnover goes to LSaS and 40% is paid out to the partner for the operation of the solution. Thus, both partners have a strong interest in ensuring that the solution works well and as many customers as possible use the software. After the software was introduced, the next step is to internationalize the solution and offer it to a larger market.

While the Market Cultivation Strategy was being drafted, the idea came up that the success of the new solution could be increased if it was not just its own salespeople selling the software, but partners selling the software as well. These distributors would be involved in a successful contract on sales. Thus, LSaS would no longer have to deal directly with the foreign business, but only targeted distribution partners would have to be found. Of course, these must be provided with information so that they can successfully sell the product. For this a corresponding partner model must be worked out, in which also the contractual affairs are regulated. This is to be done in the next step by the sales manager in consultation with the managing director.

After the idea has been completed and the Business Model, the Business Plan and the Partner Model have already been worked out, development can start. This phase will not be described further here.

An existing customer agreed to be available for testing the new software after talking with the sales manager. After the first version of the new software has been created, a test can be carried out with a real customer. The feedback can then immediately flow into the development. After the final version has been completed, this test customer will be migrated to the new system for free. For this, he makes himself available as a reference. This means that LSaS may advertise promotions for the new software with a successful implementation on that customer.

During the development phase, new web technology developers will be hired to develop the new software. In addition, the Revenue Share Agreement between LSaS and the data center operator will be prepared and signed. At the same time, the employees of LSaS and the partner are joined together to form an operating team, which provides support in operation.

In addition, a new training course will be designed to help customers learn how to operate the new software.

In order to promote the new software and make it known to a broad public, a Marketing Strategy is developed, which provides that a campaign invites all existing customers to introduce them to the new software. Furthermore, trade fair appearances are planned at national and international logistics trade fairs. In addition, a telephone acquisition company was commissioned to call additional target customers who are currently using other software and to promote the solution. Advertisements for the solution are also being advertised on the internet and the homepage of LSaS is being optimized with the help of an SEO specialist (Search Engine Optimization) in order to direct more interested customers to the corresponding page.

Before the new software can be switched completely live, adjustments to the accounting software of LSaS must also be made. The new cloud model now requires invoices to be generated monthly, dynamically based on the number of active users. For this, a new reporting and a corresponding controlling must be introduced, so that the numbers can be correctly recorded and correctly calculated. To achieve this, the revenues generated must also be shared within the Revenue Share with the data center provider and potential partners.

7.3   Result

After the first successful completion of the Business Development process, the following qualitative and quantitative results are recorded:

Qualitative:

- With the new cloud version of the software, a timely tool has been developed and successfully placed on the market.
- The old product is preserved. The development costs are shut down. Overall, the product is transferred to Cash Cow mode. Existing customers can migrate to the new platform in a transitional phase at a discounted price.
- A new, strategic partnership has been set up, which is technologically and sales-wise forward-looking.
- New internal resources for web development and operations have been built.
- The basis for a growing ecosystem around the software has been created. This will enable growth for the coming years.
- The software has been prepared for the international market and can potentially be distributed anywhere.
- The new solution is very well received by customers and is perceived as innovative.

Quantitative:

- The cloud-based Business Model has added a new flexible way of doing business with the "on-demand / pay-as-you-go" model, which provides recurring cashflow.
- The existing business can be operated more cost-effectively through the Cash Cow mode.
- Overall, sales were increased.
- In three years, a break-even is expected. This means that all investment costs for the development of the new software have already been amortized in this period.
- The company is experiencing positive staff growth.
- For the first time business was made abroad, as a first customer from the Netherlands has already introduced the new version of the software.

After successfully placing the new cloud-based solution on the market, the managing director of LSaS is conducting a Lessons Learned Session. The entire process and the actual result are reflected and recorded in writing. He states that the process as a whole was very successful and that Business Development should be a permanent component of further company development in the future. To do this, he uses a monthly Business Development Board that, in addition to him, continues to comprise the sales manager and the development manager. In addition, it is planned to regularly invite further internal or external experts to concrete topics and to bring fresh impetus to development and sales through keynote speeches. The managing director has already come up with something for the next Business Development round: he would like to develop a suitable mobile app for the logistics software and have it distributed internationally.

Interview with Björn Radde

Abstract

This chapter provides an insight into the use of Business Development at T-Systems. Björn Radde, Vice President Digital Experience, was interviewed for this purpose. He vividly describes how Business Development is used in the company to operate close to the target market. For example, he describes the T-Systems Innovation Centers, where new technologies and business models are tested together with customers.

T-Systems is a subsidiary of Deutsche Telekom and operates subsidiaries in over 20 countries worldwide. The company, headquartered in Frankfurt, currently employs more than 28,000 people. T-Systems is one of the leading consulting firms in the area of digitization and uses individual approaches to advise customers from a wide range of industries in the public and private sectors. The current focus topics are Advisory, Cloud Services, Digital Enablement, and Security.

Björn Radde is responsible for the customer experience at all digital touchpoints (web page, social media, newsletter, etc.). In addition, he is responsible for the area of social selling, active and content-driven sales via the social networks and the training of employees in this area. Here they learn how to act on LinkedIn and Twitter, for example, how to communicate effectively and with a wide reach, and how to continuously expand their network. Björn Radde is responsible for the internal Chief Tomorrow Officer program (CTO). Here, young talents from universities are accepted with a targeted question and supported with concrete research concerns in the company. In the program, for example, questions such as "How will blockchain influence our business in the future?", "Will we be equipped with chip implants in the future and how could this be put to good use?" and "How can the topic of sustainability be increased?" are addressed.

He is also responsible for the T-Systems Innovation Center in Munich. Besides this center, there are two more in Barcelona (Spain) and Utrecht (Nethalands). These are centers of innovative encounters where customers can experience the latest technology live and

© Springer Fachmedien Wiesbaden GmbH, part of Springer Nature 2023   137
A. Kohne, *Business Development*,
https://doi.org/10.1007/978-3-658-38844-7_8

work together with T-Systems specialists on creative ideas and business models. During the Corona pandemic, a virtual reality (VR) Innovation Center was created where meetings can take place with people spread all over the world. In the process, the three physical Innovation Centers and the virtual one are used for active Business Development. The goal is to find new solutions together with customers and to permanently deal with new technologies and opportunities of the market.

Andreas Kohne (AK):   What is your definition of Business Development?

Björn Radde (BR):   For me, Business Development means discovering new business areas together with customers without immediately coming up with a solution. Completely new ideas or entire business models can then emerge in this process.

To this end, for example, current technologies are examined in our Innovation Centers for their usability without immediately having a product or solution in mind. For example, a 3D-capable tablet was recently tested that allows 3D content to be viewed without the need for additional glasses. There is not yet a finished use case. But that can change in one of the next customer meetings from one moment to the next. We therefore use active technology scouting to always be at the cutting edge of what is technologically feasible and then use this knowledge to create a custom-fit solution together with the customer.

AK: How do you use Business Development at T-Systems to optimally align new products with your target groups?

BR: On the one hand, we very actively use our Innovation Centers just described to create relevant solutions with our customers. On the other hand, we use our "Market Insights". This is our own market research, which observes the market, customers and their needs and draws conclusions for our own business. In addition, we work here with a renowned external service provider who supports us in the area of market observation and trend scouting. We can then draw our conclusions from the mix of internal and external observation and adjust our strategy accordingly.

AK: Is Business Development a separate unit at your company or is it integrated into the individual departments?

BR: There is no central Business Development unit at T-Systems. Instead, the Business Development managers are directly involved in the various portfolio units, for example in the fast-growing healthcare sector. There, they work directly with customers as industry specialists.

AK: What competencies and skills have helped you in Business Development?

BR: I think the most important qualities are curiosity and being able to listen. It's about listening to what the customer wants, as well as the drive to understand and to want to learn.

AK: This fits very well with the T-Shape model (see Sect. 2.2). Are you familiar with this model and do you use it?

BR: I know the model and especially at Telekom we know the "T" very well (laughs). The colleagues in the specific areas naturally bring deep industry experience, for example in healthcare, automotive, etc., and therefore a strong middle bar. In my field, especially in digital marketing, I prefer the left and right bars to be stronger, as the middle part can be trained. Soft skills are more of a challenge here. Expertise can be acquired very quickly these days.

AK: What methods do you use to generate new ideas?

BR: In our Innovation Centers, we use design thinking to generate new ideas and arrive at solutions together with our customers. We also use hackathons at external and internal events (see Sect. 2.5.1). Internally, employees from a wide range of country organizations take part. In addition, there are "learn sessions" in which new topics are presented internally. This often results in new ideas. We also have "Deepdive Sessions" in which particularly interesting areas are explored in greater depth and employees can ask further questions. We also use classic brainstorming (see Sect. 2.5.1) to generate new ideas.

For the past two years, we've held hackathons and design thinking workshops remotely due to the pandemic. While this works, it is incredibly exhausting. While I am a very digital person, I still prefer face-to-face events for this, as I believe that events where you get creative and develop new ideas are better done together on-site.

AK: How do you test new ideas?

BR: We do a lot of testing in the "Digital" area. In the context of "Usability Test", we test our new products directly with the customer at an early stage. New web pages and campaigns are also tested. For this purpose, we use MVPs (Minimal Viable Products, cf. Sect. 2.5.5.1), i.e., very small solutions, and then develop further on the MVP. Furthermore, we have regular internal feedback loops and our customer managers collect feedback directly on site.

AK: Does T-Systems have a process for how the best ideas are transferred to further development within the company after a hackathon, design thinking workshop or other creative process?

BR: The winners of the hackathons and the results of the design thinking are processed after the events and then presented to interested customers so that the ideas can then be developed further together. The results from internal sessions are collected in a backlog and further discussed in regular sprints (see Sect. 1.7), evaluated and, if positive, further developed internally.

AK: How have you integrated permanent change and innovation into the company culture?

BR: It is still a process (laughs). The management board leads as an example. There are a lot of internal events where the board gets together and talks about it. I think it is like an evangelism that needs to be repeated often. In these meetings, there is always a call for more innovation and a call to build and develop "thought leadership" and to take this to the outside world. To this end, specialists are hired who, with a great deal of know-how and expertise, exemplify innovation on a daily basis.

AK: Do you think Business Development can help guide companies safely through crises and even strengthen them if necessary?

BR: Business Development certainly helps to react faster in a crisis. Whether a company can successfully get through a crisis depends, of course, on a wide variety of factors. If you can't change processes quickly and don't react agilely, even the best Business Development won't help you, but it will help and support you to get through crises better.

AK: How do you assess the future relevance of Business Development for companies in any industry?

BR: If I understand Business Development as the co-creation of new ideas and business models with customers, it will become more and more relevant. It will have a high importance to do Business Development properly and to be close to the customer and the market. Especially in the B2B sector. After all, we're not selling candy bars (laughs). Of course, this also applies in the B2C area and also for candy bars. I have to know whether my customers want vegan, light, or dark chocolate. So it is extremely important to listen to the customers and generate the new business or business field from that.

AK: Is there anything else you would like to say about Business Development?

BR: As a digital marketeer, social media is very important to me because it allows me to listen very closely to my customers. It's best not just to listen, but to participate in the discussion. You can listen very nicely via social listening, but if you are active and have good Business Developers actively communicating with customers on LinkedIn and Twitter, then there can be an impact that has been underestimated. I suspect that companies that do this are better than others because they are closer to the customer. Dell was the first company at the time to have a Chief Listening Officer. He had a whole command post where he could see in real time where in the world people were talking about Dell and how. They could then draw their conclusions from that and improve their products very quickly. For example, they learned that on some devices it was not possible to plug in two USB sticks at the same time. As a result, the products were adapted very quickly. Nowadays, we are one step ahead and not only listen, but also join in the discussion. This is an area where companies can do even better. Companies can also get better in the area of "co-creation" with customers (see Sect. 2.5.1.1) and develop new products together with their customers or even outsource the creative process entirely via a croudsourcing process.

This interview impressively shows how Business Development can be used to combine customer requirements and current technologies to create new business models and how Business Development works in an international company. Many thanks for the interview to Björn Radde and T-Systems.

In Six Steps to Business Development

9

Abstract

Successful businesses require rapid time-to-market products that are optimally tailored to customer needs. Business Development helps to understand the current market situation and to guide and accompany the corresponding changes. In this chapter, steps that have been described in detail in this book have been summarized again.

This book describes the theme of Business Development in its entirety. In doing so, the most important aspects are presented individually and put in a larger context. In the following, the six aspects of Business Development are briefly summarized once more:

1. *Basics:* Business Development can help you, in times of rapid change, to adapt your product portfolio to customer needs. To do this, you should make sure, with the help of an internal change management, that the necessary changes are adequately and understandably communicated and anchored in the enterprise. Furthermore, it should be kept in mind that while doing any changes in the company, or to a product or service to always inform all affected stakeholders involved early on and on a continuous basis. This is the only way to ensure a controlled project flow. Overall, you should create in your business a culture in which change does not create anxiety, but is considered something normal and necessary. This way you create and distribute market-relevant products.

2. *Organization and Process:* When integrating Business Development in your organization, you should be careful to define the role, responsibilities, and tasks of the Business Development manager. Make sure that the team (the department or the person) is accepted in the company. Also, be sure to select people to accomplish this task who meet the appropriate role profile. When implementing Business Development in your company, you can opt for a central or decentralized organizational unit. Choose the best solution for you. Continue to define a Business Development process that dictates where new ideas should

© Springer Fachmedien Wiesbaden GmbH, part of Springer Nature 2023
A. Kohne, *Business Development*,
https://doi.org/10.1007/978-3-658-38844-7_9

be developed. This will secure the quality of the new developments. Remember, however, that the process is not set in stone and should be constantly questioned and optimized.

3. *Portfolio:* Your portfolio contains all products and services that you offer to your customers. Look for a clear structure of your portfolio and sort each product into this structure. This way you have an overview of your products and can clearly classify for each product the corresponding phase in the portfolio life cycle. You need a fine-tuned controlling that helps you to define, measure, and monitor relevant product metrics. With the help of this data, you can then actively manage your products. An important task of portfolio management (which is located in Business Development) is to identify, for example, weak-wallet portfolio items, and to optimize them, either to bring them back or to remove them from the portfolio.

4. *Resources:* Be sure to build and operate a Business Development program to ensure that sufficient resources are available to you. These resources may be, for example, employee skills or financial resources. As it may be too expensive to have all resources in stock, it is a good idea to use a good mix of internal and external resources. In this way, you optimize your expenses and can react flexibly to changing market situations. If you want to increase your company's inorganic growth, you should consider mergers and acquisitions early on, because with skillful acquisitions, you can quickly gain market share or new products and employees. To monitor all of these resources and their proper use, you should set up a functioning controlling system that will assist you in managing your business with the appropriate data.

5. *Target Market:* In order to best sell your products, it is very important to know and understand your target market accurately. For this a permanent market observation is necessary. At the same time, you should segment your target market as accurately as possible in order to create an appropriate product and sales communication for each customer group. Continue to observe the opportunities that arise in the rapidly changing markets. But never forget the risks. In doing so you can ensure that you can make good decisions even in uncertainty. Also note that growth can also be achieved through targeted internationalization of the company or distribution. Many surrounding conditions and guidelines have to be considered in order to make this step successful.

6. *Marketing Strategy:* The marketing strategy is the heart of the Business Development. It defines exactly how the given product is made available to the customers. An important point here is the pricing of the product depending on the target market. Furthermore, the sales concept is defined here, which defines how your product is sold in your target market. At the same time, the partner concept is created, which ensures that strategic partners broaden your sales channels and thus reach customers who otherwise would not be reached by you. The marketing concept is also defined here. It ensures that your product is adequately promoted and publicized in your target customer segment. Finally, Business Development is also responsible for sales enablement. In doing so, you support your sales team in specific sales situations, because while launching a new product a large amount of product and sales know-how is concentrated in the Business Development team. The goal

is that the sales department is quickly able to sell and to conduct customer discussions on their own. In addition, Business Development can provide for example trainings or special sales documents.

I hope that the book has pleased you, gave you a good overview of the subject of Business Development, and is a good guidebook for your everyday business.

I wish you and your company all the best for the future and success in the ongoing, customer-oriented and forward-looking development of your products and services.

Quotes from Science and Business

Abstract

For this chapter, statements from science and business specialists were collected on the topic of Business Development. In each case, the different statements are reproduced as quotations.

After the topic of Business Development has been described in detail in this book, statements from specialists have been collected for the following chapter. They show how extensive Business Development is and how different industries assess and use Business Development.

I would like to express my gratitude to all the citers and their respective companies and universities for their comments.

Business Development is an extremely important task, especially in the real estate industry. Social developments are always reflected in real estate and its diverse uses. Anyone who organizes their company in an agile manner in this situation, reacts to new trends and consistently focuses on the needs of their customers or tenants will continue to be successful in the future. The major goal of climate neutrality, the 10-minute city, and many more topics for the future present players with major challenges and equally significant opportunities. With the right approaches to Business Development, the treasures of the future can be raised.

Dr. Marco Boksteen, Founder/Chairman of the board, Ruhrwert Immobilien und Beteiligungs GmbH and CEO Hagener Gemeinnützige Wohnungsgesellschaft mbH

Business Development is often confused with sales and closing deals. I see it as much more, as it brings together several functions. It defines the strategy for target customers and partners that fit your business strategy. It's about building and nurturing those relationships, understanding their objectives and goals, and figuring out how best to bring them together with your own. Ultimately, Business Development builds a level of trust that facilitates all inter-company transactions.

Graham Breen, Business Development & Partnerships, Innoactive GmbH

Business Development was once explained to me many years ago very simply as follows: In Business Development, you tend to work on the company—not necessarily in the company. How a company protects itself from disruptive influences or which targeted measures are crucial for further development: Business Development is supposed to identify the drivers. The results can usually be used to determine clear derivations for successfully securing the future.

Olaf Bremer, Managing Partner at projekt//partner, storeR GmbH

"Putting your ears to the rails"

Business Development is not something that happens in a quiet closet. You have to go out and know the market, customer needs and, above all, trends, interdependencies and developments.

You don't always read about that in the newspapers. Reacting quickly to changes and sometimes changing perspectives works well in networks and in cooperation with creative partners, some of whom are completely unfamiliar with the industry.

Cross innovation is my favorite answer to the challenges faced by everyone responsible for this topic.

Kai Bünseler, Managing Director, TZ Net GmbH

Stagnation—what an odious word in an economic context. After all, stagnation implies standstill, lack of ideas and fear—fear of the new and the unknown. But isn't it precisely this courage that has brought us innovations in the past? Just think of our beloved smartphones! By persevering or saying "We've always done it this way!" we would certainly not be at the point economically and technologically where we are today. So let's pause for a moment and logically come to the conclusion that only successive progress and the development of new business fields in particular will continue to enrich us with groundbreaking and milestone-setting innovations in the future. So it pays to remain curious, to understand the needs of your customers, to create added value, and to convey your corporate message in a way that is geared to your target group.

Sebastian Gresch, Account Executive, FedEx Express

Business Developers are pioneers, strategists, networkers, impulse generators, consultants—and, above all, real doers. In practice, this means more than identifying new markets, customers, and partnerships. Rather, these potentials must also be leveraged—and this can only be achieved through close collaboration with other customer-facing functions such as marketing, sales, or account and product management. Through this networking, Business Development becomes the commercial control center in the company. In the post-Covid world, this is happening right on the pulse of the times: digitally networked, technologically competent, and equipped with staying power.

Daniel Gäßler, Director Sales & Services thyssenkrupp NXT

The dear good partner.

As a software manufacturer, it is essential to operate with a well-functioning partner network. After all, the so-called channel is considered a supplier of sales and a guarantor for a more effective market penetration and thus the acquisition of end customers.

However, it becomes interesting when partner programs and concepts that have been created in advance with a lot of time and effort do not fit the respective partner. The diversity of partners can be great and thus represents a challenge.

If, on the one hand, a solution that requires little explanation "out of the box" is required, the other side demands a highly integrative solution including a high degree of technical and organizational consulting. The world in between is multi-faceted.

This is where, in addition to partner management, Business Development is needed to develop and establish a joint win-win situation for a well-functioning partnership. Of course, tools such as SWOT analysis, Business Model Canvas, business plans and, if necessary, Miller Heimann's Gold Sheet in a modified form can help.

However, my experience also shows that a high degree of flexibility is always an advantage and that rigid structures and processes rarely lead to success.

Of course, the so-called "red" thread must be included, but it has always helped to make individual agreements as well. This inevitably has consequences for the own company. Starting with various requirements for the research department of the development up to adjustments of payment modalities in the finance department. These also have to be evaluated. In general, this means a colorful bouquet of activities to launch the partner business together and successfully. From my experience, this is always an exciting and never boring task, with the dear good partner.

Christian Hanisch, Head of Business Development, Ceyoniq Technology GmbH

Challenges in Business Development:

In the context of many projects around the development of new markets by expansion of the product portfolio or by means of internationalization, many things have changed in the last decades. As an example, I would like to mention the communication strategy.

In the context of a "customer-oriented business field development", it is now more important than ever to adapt the communication strategy to the different cultures of an otherwise homogeneous target group. Whereas in the past it was possible to use country-specific communication strategies, today's multiculturalism is a challenge for Business Development in every country in order to be able to leverage the expected market potential. In today's globalized and medially fragmented world, communication strategies for international projects should therefore be geared to different cultures and communication channels and not just country-specific.

This also applies to one's own language area. For example, as recently as the end of the 1990s,s, a marketing campaign to enter the German kitchen market was met with massive protests from the Catholic Church, because it was advertised with the bon mot "Get into the devil's kitchen". Thank goodness there was no social media back then. Today, one must take care to consider the needs/demands of a multicultural society when developing the market.

Jan Hoettges, Partner, Böcker Ziemen Management Consultants GmbH & Co. KG

Business Development goes far beyond hiring a Business Development Manager. An open corporate culture, the promotion of the personal development of employees and a management that is willing to actively embrace change are essential to bring the impulses provided by BDM to life. If these conditions are met, Business Development is an incredibly exciting field that can take a company to the next level.

Lisa-Marie Ihnen, Business Development Manager, ahd GmbH & Co. KG

In our rapidly changing business environment, the role of Business Development becomes crucial. Effective Business Development is the key ingredient for digital transformation and new business creation.

Dirk Kanngiesser, CEO Cryptowerk Corp. and Managing Director TU capital

Business Development today should be immersive. It needs a good balance and especially a good communication between the contexts and systems, between plan and experiment, between model and prototype, between tolerance of ambiguity and coherence. But perhaps it also needs a new terminology. Business or "being busy" as a conceptualization still has the etymological of being busy—a possibly undirected busy being or even a busy being dedicated to an end in itself.

We should start searching for a new terminology.

Dr. Martin Kiel, the black frame. think tank.

Innovation needs a playground. A playground that offers employees from different areas of the company a shared, protected space in which they can try out new things. This playground must be protected in terms of time, i.e., a fixed quota of working hours must be available for experimenting and playing. The normal work routine and business-as-usual have no place here. And the playground must be financially secure. It must allow people to try things out first—to experiment and play. What is then played? That depends on the company in question. A journal club in which current studies are discussed together is just as appropriate as trying out new technologies and devices—from augmented and virtual reality to blockchain and quantum computing. Per se, everything is worth trying out first. So go play!

Dr. Sebastian Klöß, Head of Consumer Technology & AR/VR, Bitkom

Strategic Business Development is increasingly becoming a decisive success factor in the insurance and banking environment. In the past, the focus here was often on traditional product sales, e.g., at the bank counter, via intermediaries, or using the bank's own direct sales channels. In the B2B2C environment, partners now increasingly expect the intelligent and flexible integration of relevant white-label offerings ("embedded offerings") at their point of sale. Since these offerings should subsequently be perceived by the end customer as a single entity, a deep understanding of the partner is essential.

The task of Business Development here goes far beyond a pure sales approach. In addition to in-depth knowledge of the target industry, the respective partner, and its end customers, the focus is on developing and operationalizing a common strategic vision. The requirements for products, processes, and digitization are then derived from this vision and regularly adapted to current developments and future opportunities. Strategic Business Development creates the framework for a continuous process and actively supports the partner in operating successfully on the market in the long term.

Gregor Mandt, Senior Project Manager Strategy, HDI AG

Business Development means to be committed to the strategic and operational development of the company, to open up new business areas, and to implement new business ideas.

In doing so, it is necessary to penetrate the technical reference and to fathom the value creation processes of the acting actors. The answer to the crucial question is to be found: How can the performance of one's own company be brought in, so that a quantifiable profit is created for the customer.

If this question is answered and good products are added, then the way is paved for positive development.

In the course of Business Development, the contacts are also established to proclaim this message effectively to the new market.

Michael Mundt, Senior Business Development Manager, Esri Deutschland GmbH

With Business Development, companies can provide answers to questions their customers never thought they had, and later those customers say, "This is exactly the solution I've been waiting for". So Business Development is too important to leave to just a few people in the company. It is the responsibility of the entire team of marketing, sales, development, controlling, etc. and must be initiated, supported and led by top management in the role of coach.

Prof. Dr. Christian Müller-Roterberg, Ruhr West University of Applied Science

Customer-oriented business field development for successful companies from the perspective of a Business Development manager:

What qualifies me to be a Business Development manager?

My colleagues like to refer to me as a "glue code", a solution finder and an interface manager. These three designations describe my various tasks, which I am fortunate to perform in a successful company with a trusting corporate culture. This company offers people an innovation-promoting and familiar platform. Here, many IT enthusiasts realize their ideas and visions. I bring people together who increase the value, efficiency and benefit of companies through their individual expertise in collaboration. For me, this means to actively contribute to the development of the company and the customers and to connect the departments.

To be allowed to be who I am and to respect others as they are and to provide security, trust and ultimately success with this consistent style. To be an honorable businessperson while promoting inherent principles and exemplifying commitment and behavior in word and deed to the goals of the company and customers. To contribute personal strengths and competencies to the team and to compensate for weaknesses with a success-oriented team. Serve all colleagues, partners, and customers equally and make their lives a little easier through collaborative and innovative support.

True cross-departmental, interdisciplinary, collaborative, trusting, loyal, and smart collaboration with the right mindset, the right triad of methods, processes, and tools. An exemplary mindset might be the following: Always thinking of the bridge from science to practice and acting according to the management concept "The fifth discipline—The Art and Practice of the Learning Organization" by Peter M. Senge (cf. [42]):

1. Personal mastery (intrinsic motivation and diligence),
2. Mental models (openness and honesty),
3. Shared vision (identity, purpose, and benefits),
4. Team learning (culture of dialogue),
5. Systems Thinking (interdependencies and interactions).

Plan and execute value-added activities through concrete management and support processes.

Talking to everyone at eye level and not taking any statements that seem negative at first glance personally, but always examining them self-critically or, in other words, having "a thick skin". When things get stressful, always keep in mind that it is not a matter of human life, as is the case, for example, with the profession of a doctor. As a joy bearer to serve my fellow men with advice and action in an exemplary, honest and effective way. To be a dolphin in the shark tank of the real economy and to make this a strong unique selling point. If necessary, using an equalizer in one's brain to filter the signals and sounds received so that one extracts objective, factual and useful information from a conversation. Being generous with praise and gentle with criticism.

Charalambos Panagiotidis, Business Development & Operations Manager, itemis AG

As a company with a well-run operational business, it can be easy to neglect the development of business areas. With this comes the risk of losing market relevance and suddenly being forced to take drastic action. In a digitalizing world with ever shorter innovation cycles, this risk is becoming ever greater, correspondingly shortening the life expectancy of companies. Business Development is the systematic answer to this risk. In our own past as a company and also in the more detailed analysis of our market environment, we have repeatedly recognized the importance of Business Development as a long-term success factor.

Dr. Gero Presser, Managing Director, QuinScape GmbH

Successful business field development and Business Development engagements are subject to additional requirements in the public sector and need a special "wide view" beyond the individual customer or department.

The public sector market is characterized by diverse, networked "center structures", all of which are interdependent, and no single public sector customer has final decision-making authority.

Buying centers, such as the procurement office of the Federal Ministry of the Interior, in which aggregated requirements are bundled and awarded contracts. Cooperation networks at the state level (e.g., in the area of justice and police administration) Policy setting centers, such as the IT Planning Council and the Federal Chancellery shared delivery centers, such as the Federal IT Center and numerous municipal data centers.

The main drivers of the public sector market are always national and supranational (EU) legislation. This complexity and interdependencies must be included, evaluated, and adapted at an early stage in a Business Development in the public sector. This makes BDM activities time-consuming, but also exciting.

Johannes Rosenboom, Vice President Sales, Business Development and Marketing - Business Line Public Sector, Materna Information & Communications SE

Take the time to grind your axe
In management workshops, I like to work with a quote from Abraham Lincoln: "If I have eight hours to cut down a tree, I'll use six hours to grind the axe". This analogy beautifully sums up the idea of Business Development: to be successful and endure as a company in the marketplace, I must always be curious and well informed. I should give strategic work and information gathering the priority it deserves. Means: finding synergies and solutions, recognizing potential where others only see obstacles—identifying successful strategies, analyzing them, abstracting them, and transferring them to my own business situation.

Ben Unruh, Chief Business Development Officer, Z-Systems GmbH

Especially during the first contact with customers, it is important to find out what they actually need. Because that is not necessarily what they want. When dealing with new technologies, expectations, objectives, feasibility, and cost-effectiveness must be reconciled together with the customer. The better this succeeds, the more convincing the result.

Robin Wenk, Co-Founder, Lightshape GmbH & Co. KG

References

1. B. Avak. *Variant Management of Modular Product Families in the Market Phase*. Fortschritt-Berichte VDI / 16: Technik und Wirtschaft. VDI-Verlag, 1994.
2. Richard Banfield, C Todd Lombardo, and Trace Wax. *Design Sprint: A Practical Guidebook for Building Great Digital Products*. O'Reilly Media, Inc., 2015.
3. A. Beerel. *Leadership and Change Management*. SAGE Publications, 2009.
4. Edward Blackwell. *How to Prepare a Business Plan: Create Your Strategy; Forecast Your Finances; Produce That Persuasive Plan*. Kogan Page Publishers, 2011.
5. Steve Blank. Perfection By Subtraction - The Minimum Feature Set. Zugriff am 31. Mai 2022 from https://steveblank.com/2010/03/04/perfection-by-subtraction-the-minimum-feature-set/, 2010.
6. Jörg Breithut. Virale Werbefallen - Pril schmeckt nach Hähnchen. Access: 31. May 2022 from https://www.spiegel.de/netzwelt/web/virale-werbefallen-pril-schmeckt-nach-haehnchen-a-756532.html, 2011.
7. R.F. Bruner and J.R. Perella. *Applied Mergers and Acquisitions, University Edition*. Wiley Finance. Wiley, 2016.
8. Patrick J Brunet. The alchemy of growth: Practical insights for building the enduring enterprise. *Library Journal*, 124(8):90–91, 1999.
9. T. Buzan and B. Buzan. *The Mind Map Book*. Mind set. BBC Active, 2006.
10. R.J. Chapman. *Simple Tools and Techniques for Enterprise Risk Management*. The Wiley Finance Series. Wiley, 2011.
11. Anne Conzemius and Jan O'Neill. *The power of SMART goals: Using goals to improve student learning*. Solution Tree Press, 2009.
12. Haluk Demirkan and Jim Spohrer. T-shaped innovators: Identifying the right talent to support service innovation. *Research-Technology Management*, 58(5):12–15, 2015.
13. L. Downes and P. Nunes. *Big Bang Disruption: Strategy in the Age of Devastating Innovation*. Penguin Publishing Group, 2014.
14. Gartner. Gartner Hype Cycle. Access: 31. May 2022 from https://www.gartner.com/en/research/methodologies/gartner-hype-cycle, 2022.
15. Daniel Goleman. *Emotional Intelligence*. Bantam, 2006.
16. Mark Hatch. *The maker movement manifesto: Rules for innovation in the new world of crafters, hackers, and tinkerers*. McGraw-Hill Education New York, 2014.

© Springer Fachmedien Wiesbaden GmbH, part of Springer Nature 2023
A. Kohne, *Business Development*,
https://doi.org/10.1007/978-3-658-38844-7

17. Bob Hayes and Kathleen Kotwica. *Bring your own device (BYOD) to work: Trend report*. Newnes, 2013.
18. Christian Homburg. *Marketingmanagement: Strategie-Instrumente-Umsetzung-Unternehmensführung*. Springer-Verlag, 2016.
19. S. Horowitz and T.S. Poynter. *The Freelancer's Bible: Everything You Need to Know to Have the Career of Your Dreams-On Your Terms*. Workman Publishing Company, 2012.
20. David E Hussey. *Strategic management: from theory to implementation*. Routledge, 2007.
21. M. Johnson. *Winning The War for Talent: How to Attract and Keep the People Who Make Your Business Profitable*. Wiley, 2014.
22. Spencer Johnson. *Who moved my cheese*. Random House, 2015.
23. H. Kehal. *Outsourcing and Offshoring in the 21st Century: A Socio-Economic Perspective: A Socio-Economic Perspective*. Gale virtual reference library. Idea Group Pub., 2006.
24. W.C. Kim and R. Mauborgne. *Blue Ocean Strategy, Expanded Edition: How to Create Uncontested Market Space and Make the Competition Irrelevant*. Harvard Business School Press. Harvard Business School Press, 2015.
25. Andreas Kohne and Volker Wehmeier. *Hackathons: From Idea to Successful Implementation*. Springer Nature, 2020.
26. Frank W Liou. *Rapid prototyping and engineering applications: a toolbox for prototype development*. Crc Press, 2007.
27. Heike Lorenz. Innovative Geschäftsmodelle von ADD-ON bis AUCTION. Access: 31. May 2022 from https://das-unternehmerhandbuch.de/innovative-geschaeftsmodelle-von-add-on-bis-auction/, 2014.
28. Fred A Manuele. The plan-do-check-act concept (pdca). *Advanced Safety Management Focusing on Z10 and Serious Injury Prevention*, pages 33–43, 2007.
29. Dieter Frey Marit Gerkhardt. Erfolgsfaktoren und psychologische hintergründe in veränderungsprozessen, entwicklung eines integrativen psychologischen modells. *OrganisationsEntwicklung*, April 2006.
30. R. Masterson and D. Pickton. *Marketing: An Introduction*. SAGE Publications, 2010.
31. Á. Medinilla. *Agile Kaizen: Managing Continuous Improvement Far Beyond Retrospectives*. BusinessPro collection. Springer Berlin Heidelberg, 2014.
32. Anand Narasimhan and Jean-Louis Barsoux. Leadership development - what everyone gets wrong about change management. *Harvard Business Review*, Nov 2017.
33. Alexander Osterwalder and Yves Pigneur. *Business model generation: a handbook for visionaries, game changers, and challengers*. John Wiley & Sons, 2010.
34. Gary P Pisano. *Creative construction: The DNA of sustained innovation*. PublicAffairs, 2019.
35. Hasso Plattner, Christoph Meinel, and Ulrich Weinberg. *Design thinking*. Springer, 2009.
36. G. Ramesh. *The Ace Of Soft Skills: Attitude, Communication And Etiquette For Success*. Pearson Education, 2010.
37. Martin Reeves, Sandy Moose, and Thijs Venema. BCG Classics Revisited: The Growth Share Matrix. Access: 31. May 2022 from https://www.bcgperspectives.com/content/articles/corporate_strategy_portfolio_management_strategic_planning_growth_share_matrix_bcg_classics_revisited/, 2016.
38. Thomas Reichmann. *Controlling: Concepts of Management Control, Controllership, and Ratios*. Springer-Verlag Berlin Heidelberg, 1997.
39. E. Ries. *The Lean Startup: How Today's Entrepreneurs Use Continuous Innovation to Create Radically Successful Businesses*. Crown Publishing Group, 2011.
40. Everett M Rogers. *Diffusion of innovations*. Simon and Schuster, 2010.

41. Materna Information & Communications SE. Die Zukunft digitaler Geschäftsmodelle. Access: 31. May 2022 from https://www.materna.de/Microsite/Monitor/DE/2021-03/Management-und-Strategie/digitale-geschaeftsmodelle/digitale-geschaeftsmodelle_node.html, 2022.
42. Peter M Senge. The fifth discipline. *Measuring Business Excellence*, 1997.
43. S. Sinek. *Start with Why: How Great Leaders Inspire Everyone to Take Action*. Penguin Publishing Group, 2009.
44. P. Stone. *Make Marketing Work for You: Boost Your Profits with Proven Marketing Techniques*. How to books (Oxford, England).: Small business. How To Books, 2001.
45. Michael L Tushman and Charles A O'Reilly III. Ambidextrous organizations: Managing evolutionary and revolutionary change. *California management review*, 38(4):8–29, 1996.
46. R.V. Vargas. *Practical Guide to Project Planning*. ESI International Project Management Series. CRC Press, 2007.
47. C. Wilson. *Brainstorming and Beyond: A User-Centered Design Method*. Elsevier Science, 2013.
48. Fred Wilson. The freemium business model. *A VC Blog, March*, 23, 2006.
49. XPLANE. Customer Empathy Map. Access: 31. May 2022 from http://www.xplane.com, 2016.

Index

© Springer Fachmedien Wiesbaden GmbH, part of Springer Nature 2023
A. Kohne, *Business Development*,
https://doi.org/10.1007/978-3-658-38844-7

Printed in the United States
by Baker & Taylor Publisher Services